Aspects of History

Issue Fourteen

First published in 2023 by Aspects of History.

Contents

From the Editor

This is the first issue of 2023, and the year has started with Germany reluctantly acquiescing to Ukrainian requests for tank support in their war with Russia. At the time of writing, 14 tanks have been promised, although it is likely wise to believe their involvement in the conflict when we see them cross the border. The argument German apologists have made is that it is historical guilt that has meant they have been hesitant in backing Ukraine in the life-or-death struggle against the Russians. I find this historical hand-wringing unpersuasive. If history teaches us anything, it is that we must stand up to aggressors, not appease them. Much of the fighting has been described as 'barbaric', as Russians take the fight beyond the Ukrainian army to civilians. The word 'medieval' has been used, but as Ian Mortimer passionately argues that word is being abused. He is our lead feature as I chatted with the bestselling historian on the wondrous age that is the Medieval period.

Perhaps we should not be surprised at German military deficiencies? As Peter H. Wilson explains, that Teutonic front is more hollow than we imagined. His masterly new book perhaps explains, at least in part, why the Battle of Stalingrad was lost. Iain MacGregor whose fantastic book of the battle has attracted rave reviews, and writes for us in a month where we've seen the 80th anniversary of Paulus' surrender.

In this month's issue we have a piece from Nigel Biggar. I was disturbed to learn that his book had been 'cancelled' (his contract was quite literally cancelled) by his first publisher because of unspecified 'public feeling'. If we're at the stage when publishers are dropping books because they assume some will not like them we really are in an unhealthy state. I may take issue with many authors' slant, but I would argue strongly that they be published. It is pleasing to see his book become so successful. At Aspects of History we have featured writers on both sides of the debate when it comes to empire and colonialism, and we'll continue to do so.

The Aspects of History Podcast continues to peak month on month, and there is plenty of great content which includes: a two-part special on the trial and execution of Charles I from Mark Turnbull; Gavin Mortimer's take on the BBC's SAS Rogue Heroes, Gary Sheffield talking World War One, and Peter Hughes on the state of history today. I do hope you can listen – you'll find it wherever you get your podcasts.

We continue to offer Author Platforms on our website for historians, historical novelists, academics, and students to write about their books and history in an ongoing way. In addition, we can provide publishing and promotional services to assist authors and would-be authors – from pitch to publication and beyond. If you are a member of an historical society or creative writing group, then do get in touch.

If you are interested in finding out more, please visit our website at aspectsofhistory.com, follow us on Twitter @aspectshistory, or email me at editor@aspectsofhistory.com. I am always happy to hear from readers and writers alike. This continues to be as much your magazine as ours.

Oliver Webb Carter
Editor & Co-Founder

Why the Middle Ages Matter: Ian Mortimer Interview

Ian Mortimer is one of our foremost Medieval historians, and has written biographies Edward III, Roger Mortimer and Henry IV. His Time-Traveller Guides covering Medieval, Elizabethan and Restoration England have sold in their droves, and he takes a unique approach to history. He recently met with our editor, and they chatted when the Middle Ages begin and end, Edward III and today's approach to history.

Ian, having just finished *Medieval Horizons: Why the Middle Ages Matter*, I was a bit of a sceptic about the Middle Ages before I started this book, but you've turned me. There are two or three authors that you take issue with in what they've said about the Middle Ages, and there are assumptions that you're challenging throughout, which are best summed up in the words of Marsellus Wallace from Pulp Fiction, where he states he's going to get "medieval on his ass."

Thank you very much for asking me to chat but I'm even happier to hear that I might have turned you. The book is about, to my mind as a historian who's dealt with Middle Ages for such a long time, blindingly obvious things, and yet I seem to be alone in thinking they're blindingly obvious.

"I'm going to get medieval on your ass" is now in the Oxford English Dictionary. Who would have thought it? It's come to stand for backwardness and for brutality. When I was writing about Elizabethan England 15 years ago, I discovered that nobody had done as much for torture as the Elizabethans in England. Traditionally, we do not torture people for political purposes, but the Elizabethans looked past that and of course introduced torture. So, what Marsellus Wallace should really have said is, I'm going to get Elizabeth on your ass. But doesn't have the same ring, does it?

The idea that it's brutal and backward; and the number of times we hear the Taliban described as medieval, it did wear away at me. You mentioned two or three authors who I do take issue with. All three are established professors of history and that is why I chose those three. And I could have chosen dozens, if not hundreds of other writers who've expressed very much the same view that essentially our ideas of change are technological and technology based, as opposed to anything else causing social change. I think if we just look back over the last 1000 years, so much of our change has got nothing to do with technology. It seems to me an obvious and necessary step to alert people to how much our change is not technological, and rooted in different triggers in society and demography and the weather.

When do the Middle Ages start and end?

The idea of a 'middle age' really comes from Petrarch. I don't know of anybody before Petrarch who was writing in the late 14th century, but he referred to the times between the fall of Rome and his own time as a 'dark age', and that idea grew. I can't say it convinced everybody, because you don't find anybody else referring to this 'dark age' until later in the 15th century. The term 'The Middle Ages' or the 'Medieval' period between the fall of Rome and our 'own time' you find from the 1570s, 1580s. The term 'middle age', or Middle Ages to describe between the fall of Rome and Elizabethan England. Initially, they just refer to the Middle Age. Now, from a modern perspective, we look at so many areas of change in that 16th century period that it's very difficult to have an absolute correct date for the end of the Middle Ages. My wife and I always joke the Middle Ages ended about 3:30 in the afternoon on the 22nd August 1485, when Richard III lost his head and his horse at Bosworth.

Isn't that very Anglo-centric to concentrate on the Battle of Bosworth? Those in Italy wouldn't have cared about that, would they?

Absolutely - likewise for the start of the Middle Ages. There's a difference there because if you're in Italy describing the beginning of the Middle Ages, you'd say, "well, the fall of Roman 476AD," whereas from an English or British point of view, you'd say the withdrawal of the Roman legions and the collapse of Roman authority in around 410/420AD. The thing is, why have a label? You only need the label if you're using it to a certain end. What are you trying to get across by using these terms? I have always found it very useful to use Shakespeare as a historical benchmark, and because Shakespeare knew nothing of the technological impulses that have led to us having a technological mindset in the modern world. I thought what I would do was contrast early 11th century with Shakespeare's time, so the 11th century with the 16th century. Now, most of that is medieval. Very few people think the years the 1590s are medieval, but for the purposes I wanted to get across, I went up to 1600 and I had Shakespeare in my mind.

I had the invention of the telescope and the microscope in my mind, which are both around 1590/1600, because those advance our horizons enormously and until those lenses really had done that, nothing was, on a technological basis, expanding our horizons. Ships obviously had developed and allowed us to go around the world but that metaphorical horizon the geographers allowed us to see is really true throughout this medieval period. And then when we get to that technological change, the beginning of the age of science and the scientific revolution in the 17th century, then I thought that was a point at which to compare and contrast. What I really want people to do is concentrate on everything before 1600, so hence my Middle Ages in this book goes all the way up to 1600. Normally you'll find me saying the Middle Ages in this country end with the dissolution of the monasteries and the first break from Rome.

And so we start with 1000, not the Norman Invasion?

No, because I do want to defocus or lose this. I'm an English historian, so therefore virtually every source I'm really familiar with is English and origin or English related. But I did want to broaden people's eyes to it's not just about England. the book is going to be published in Greece and none of my books have been published in Greece before. I was thinking, "oh, God. I didn't really think about Greece in terms of the Middle Ages." There's a real failure of my imagination to look to the other parts of southern Europe besides Spain and the Reconquista and Italy, but I've wanted to expand ideas and therefore I took the thing back to the early 11th century also, because even in this country, that Norman invasion did really make quite a lot of profound changes. William the Conqueror came here with the idea he's going to get rid of slavery, that slavery was a bad thing. Saxons thought slavery was a good thing, so that in itself, the 11th century changes are ones I wanted to bring into the mix.

The Black Death was rather an important *development.* I use that word advisedly.

It's a bit of an understatement. I have described it as the most important thing that's happened in recorded history. The only times anybody has ever corrected me on that is to add, "in Europe." Of course, if you're in certain parts of the world, there have been more devastating moments. If you're in Mexico, you might say that the arrival of Cortez and his clan was a bit of a devastating moment. For Europeans, it's the most extraordinary cataclysmic event, but there are silver linings to it. And a lot of the breakdown of serfdom is due to the economic opportunities of the Black Death. Very simply, if you got x number of assets and you halve the number of people who own them, well, even the people at the bottom of your social hierarchy are going to benefit in some small way. Likewise, the people who are exploiting those who are now dead, they are going to suffer.

We do actually see a significant lessening of inequality in this period. Inequality is one of those difficult historical questions I have tried to tackle. The Black Death is one where you can see shifts of income inequality getting better and unfortunately getting worse again in the 16th century. The Black Death, it must have been hell to live through. As we now know, over 40% of the population dying in seven months. You couldn't really have dealt with that and it not have some psychological impact. That your view of the world and how the goodwill of God himself must really have come under strain. For those who did survive, there were economic and social benefits and more of their children survived. It must have been traumatic, really.

If you throw in war and fighting and with our understanding of mental health nowadays, I've got visions of 80% of the population walking around traumatised with PTSD.

Absolutely. When you also think how many kids they're losing in childbirth or in infant mortality and the huge oppression of the hierarchy of society, even if you are lucky, if you are low down in that pecking order, you're going to be traumatised most of the time.

Do you think there's a person who best represents the Medieval period?

The characters that come to mind are people who basically seized their age and shook it by the scruff of their neck. And by suggesting characters like Peter Abelard or Edward III of England, you're looking at individuals who are so remarkable, they're not typical. So, they don't represent the Middle Ages in terms of they embody the Middle Ages, their careers embody, really, the changes that we now associate with the Middle Ages.

Edward III's idea of kingship: He took a world which was basically a series of kingdoms and a king with authority over his people. And when he left this world in 1377, he'd left a new vision of kingship, whereby kings operate with their elected representatives in Parliament, whereby they are as symbolic as they are directly in control. When we think in terms of Big Ben, symbol of the United Kingdom, I suppose, these days. Well, that tower is based on the site of the Edward Bell Tower, the bell that he created in the tower at Westminster Palace. In many ways that symbol of the United Kingdom goes back to Edward III and his impact on parliament. Windsor Castle was virtually entirely rebuilt by him. The idea that a king should lead his people in battle and be merciless to his enemies and yet listen to his subjects through parliament, his ideas of dynamic kingship, and throughout his 50-year reign, he was his own prime minister.

Remember, he is one of the people who really does embody the challenges of the Middle Ages. How do you take what is wrong and set it right in the 14th century?

You can look at characters like that all the way through the Middle Ages. People who grappled with really meaty problems and contributed to the development of our culture, our constitution, and I think if I were to pick people, I would use them as a vehicle to describe their impact in the Middle Ages and expose the Middle Ages through them.

You write about the way we look back on history with our own values. And you've mentioned Richard III, he's certainly one who gets judged by modern standards. Do you think this is a failing of history at the moment from historians in there seems to be a real trend for current day values being applied to the past?

I think it goes both ways and I think there are very few people in the middle of this fundamental problem. There are professors of history I know who insist in an academic purism, which means that you only judge people by the standards of their own time. There's one person who I will not name, who sticks in my mind particularly for this, who is adamant that we should judge Colston as a good man because he was good to his city. We have no right to judge him out of the spirit of his time. I find this is ivory tower sort of history, and you have to recognise that you have an audience as a historian. It is not just about you understanding the past, if you're a historian, it's about you being able to relate the meaning of that past to the people around you, to whom you have a responsibility. Now, the people around you have their own values and there's no point in them understanding whether Colston was a good guy in the early 18th century.

They can presume that because they put up a statue to him in the 19th century. The relevance is, what can you learn from this? What is meaningful to us about understanding the past? I think that the alternative point of view that we judge by today's standards and that we condemn everybody in the past because they had different standards from us is equally absurd. The fact is, we are doing a triangulated operation. When we look at history, we are taking the past and using evidence. We are exploring what happened then and it's meaning for us now. But the triangulation is it goes through the historian. So it's not just the past and the present, it's the past to the historian and the historian to the present. Now, if the historian can't engage with a debate in both directions, is he or she really doing her job properly? The fact is, you have to balance these things. I think if you try and apologise for the past, you're on a hiding to nothing. I think if you try and make up for the indignities of past centuries, you're on a hiding to nothing, unless it's the other day, in which case, of course, has a different matter.

When you're looking back centuries and trying to right the wrongs of the 16th and 17th centuries, well, why choose those centuries rather than the 11th, 12th or the ancient world. Look back at slavery and Roman times if we're going to go there. That's a concept of dominion, where the slave owners were able to treat their slaves in the most appalling ways possible, throwing them alive into pools of Moray Eels to be eaten alive. I just do not think that one answer to that question is sufficient. You have to look at this triangulation. The historian has to understand how people were viewed at the time and relate that in a reasonable way to modern world, but also be aware of how standards and expectations have changed. If we don't do that with the sensitivity in both directions, what is the point of understanding the past properly? And what is the point of talking to people today if they don't want to listen about how the past was? We don't learn anything. We're just going to lay our judgments on the past and say they're all wrong.

Ian Mortimer's latest book is *Medieval Horizons: Why the Middle Ages Matter*. He is the bestselling author of *The Time Traveller's Guide to Medieval England*. You can hear an extended version of this interview on the Aspects of History Podcast.

Iron & Blood: The German War Machine, by Peter H. Wilson

The capacity for war is assumed to be in the German psyche since time immemorial, but it's a little more complex than that as historian Peter H. Wilson explains.

China might seem an odd location from which to reflect on German militarism, but two noted incidents from the Boxer Rebellion of 1900 nicely illustrate the diverging interpretations. The first occurred on 22 June in the wake of the first, failed attempt by the international force to break the siege of the diplomatic legations in Beijing. Hard-pressed by Boxers and Chinese regulars, the relief column under the British Admiral Edward Seymour found their retreat blocked by a fortified arsenal outside Tientsin (Tianjin). Seymour ordered 'The Germans to the front' to reinforce the units already detached to clear the way.

The episode was swiftly celebrated in a magnificent canvas by Carl Röchling, one of Germany's leading history painters, which shows blue-coated Royal Marines standing aside to allow their white-clad German counterparts to advance ahead. Widely reproduced at the time, the image symbolised that Germany had arrived on the global stage as a country to be reckoned with, not by the Chinese who were (unfairly) despised, but by the leading imperial powers, including not least Britain, possessor of history's largest empire. Röchling's painting celebrated what can be described as the positive interpretation of German martial qualities which has persisted, even after the defeats in the two world wars, in the widely held belief that the country possesses a unique 'genius for war'.

The second incident occurred barely a month later as Kaiser Wilhelm II addressed a much larger German expeditionary force as it set sail from Bremerhaven on 27 July to launch a renewed effort to rescue the diplomats. Signalling a clear intent to punish China for its audacity, the Kaiser invoked the memory of Attila by instructing his troops to 'take no prisoners' in clear breach of The Hague Convention he had signed only the year before. This 'Hun Speech' featured prominently in British propaganda during the two world wars, reflecting an equally deeply seated negative view of German militarism as excessive, and the belief that the country had, at some point in its history, deviated from normal, civilised development down its own 'special path' leading inevitably to total war and the Holocaust.

As is so often the case with history, neither incident was entirely as it seemed. The British Royal Marines participated in the assault of the Chinese arsenal, attacking from one side while the Germans struck another. Likewise, while the German expeditionary force indeed behaved barbarously – even its commander was embarrassed at the extent of his soldiers' looting – the other contingents from Britain, France, Italy, Austria-Hungary, Russia, Japan, and the USA were not much better, and in some cases worse.

Neither the positive tradition nor the critical perspective is wholly wrong, but both distort our understanding of what was happening, and of how the German experience compares to that elsewhere. While differing in their moral verdict, both interpretations see German military history as the inexorable rise of Prussia leading directly to the two world wars. This path was supposedly pre-determined by the country's geo-political situation in the heart of Europe which left it surrounded by hostile neighbours. Germans, it is widely believed, were somehow naturally predisposed to aggressive wars from fear of encirclement and from a desire to expand their 'living space'.

After Austria allegedly failed to provide the necessary leadership, Prussia forged German unity in a sequence of rapid, successful wars 1864-71. Their outcome tidied up the map of Central Europe, merging the smaller German states into a new Prussian-dominated empire which excluded Austria. These military successes confirmed what many believed was a pattern already established by a series of Prussian warrior kings from the Hohenzollern family, starting with the 'Great Elector' Frederick William (ruled 1640-88) and continuing most notably with his great grandson, Frederick II 'the Great (r.1740-86).

Operationally, German wars had to be *Blitzkriege* (lightning wars) to win quick and decisive victories before their enemies could combine their superior numbers against them. German armed forces allegedly strove for technical proficiency and technological superiority to gain a comparative advantage over their more numerous foes. To achieve this, it is widely believed that the armed forces were entrusted to professionals operating largely beyond political control, all with fatal consequences for German society and wider European peace

This sequence is largely the product of later nineteenth century thinking which became fixed in the aftermath of 1945 and has trapped the wider and longer story in an anachronistic and teleological framework. Militarism has been integral to the German past and has shaped how Germans have conducted wars, but that it was neither an end destination, nor a single trajectory of development.

It makes little sense to use the current German frontiers to frame analysis, not least because historic Prussia is now split between Poland and Russia. Moreover, we need to shed anachronistic ideas about national characteristics as supposedly timeless and determined by only language and culture. Germans never possessed a singular, coherent 'way of war', nor can their military history be read entirely through Prussia's experience. Today's Germany was indeed partly forged through violence, but warfare was also important in shaping Austria and Switzerland in often surprising ways, while the relative significance of conflict can only be gauged when military history is integrated with the wider story of these countries' pasts.

Starting in the sixteenth century allows us to follow Germany, Austria, and Switzerland from their origins in shared political space of the Holy Roman Empire at a point when European warfare changed profoundly. Though medieval Europe was not short on conflict, wars were usually intermittent and localised. The later fifteenth century saw the emergence of mechanisms for mobilising and directing resources in a more sustained and coordinated manner. Importantly for German history, this was not achieved by the creation of a single, national state, but through collective, multilateral structures, whereby each principality or territory was responsible for contributing to common defence.

Autonomy, not centralisation, has remained the primary political characteristic into the twentieth century and re-emerged from the two world wars in modernised form as the federalism enshrined in the German, Austrian, and Swiss republics. While individual German monarchs, princes, and lesser authorities pursued wars and feuds into the eighteenth century, the broader orientation of the Holy Roman Empire was defensive. German participation in wars beyond their own frontiers was invariably in partnership with other allies. Swiss security was also collective, and while they ceased attacking its neighbours after 1515, their subsequent neutrality was directly linked to providing other European powers with soldiers; something which persists in much reduced form in the presence of the Swiss Papal Guard.

Moreover, Prussia was not the leading 'German' military power until the later nineteenth century. Until then, the Austrian Habsburg monarchy always had a larger army and was still seen as a more desirable model by many within Central Europe and beyond. Thanks to its possessions in Italy and Croatia, the Habsburgs were also the leading German naval power into the 1880s and remained ranked seventh (ahead of Russia) in 1914, whilst the rapid expansion of the imperial German battlefleet from the late 1890s ensured that was now second only to Britain's Royal Navy.

Austria, not Prussia, was the primary aggressor operating from Central Europe prior to the 1860s and the only one capable of making war on its own account, though frequently dragging much of the Empire with it. The Austrians still performed creditably in their joint war together with Prussia against Denmark in 1864, and it was widely expected that they would triumph when the Prussians engineered a showdown two years later to determine mastery over the smaller German states.

Though Prussia and its smaller German allies displayed many qualities, their victory over France in 1870-1 was also far from a foregone conclusion. Despite capturing Napoleon III and most of the French regular army by September 1870, the new republican regime waged a 'people's war' against the invaders. The French were soon forced to make peace, but their unexpected refusal to do so earlier left the now united Germany's military leadership haunted by the spectre that future wars might slide into prolonged attritional struggles they could not win.

Simultaneously, their successes over Denmark, Austria, and France convinced most observers that the German commanders had mastered the art of war. Countries as diverse as Chile, China, Japan, and the USA adopted elements of Prussian doctrine, practice, equipment, uniforms, and military culture such as music and marching songs. Concern for their jealously guarded professional prestige led the German generals to consistently underestimate the dangerous odds they would face in a war. They were not alone in this, as much of Austria-Hungary's military leadership shared the same delusion by 1914.

Despite defeat in the First World War, German officers largely refused to abandon their obsession with achieving a swift victory. That was the only 'lightning' element to Blitzkrieg which never existed as a coherent strategy because the General Staff largely lacked a strategy at all, thinking primarily in operational and especially tactical terms. Less than a tenth of the army was motorised during the Second World War, while the inability of the dysfunctional Nazi state to standardise created logistical nightmare. Eighty-five percent of the vehicles had broken down within first five months of the invasion of the Soviet Union in 1941, while the advance was actually slower than Napoleon's equally ill-fated attack in 1812.

The unprecedented scale of both world wars ensured that the consequences of these defeats were felt far beyond Germany. Among the many reasons behind the failures, the disregard of diplomacy ranks highly. Diplomatic options which might have rendered conflict unnecessary altogether were frequently ignored, while the country twice embarked on major wars without a clear link between the intended purpose of victory and the means to achieve it. The interests of real and potential allies were repeatedly ignored both prior to hostilities and once these had begun. The elusiveness of the desired swift, easy victory prompted the country's leadership to widen each conflict, thereby merely adding to the number of enemies and stacking the odds further against them. Far from representing an ideal model of how to win a modern war, the German experience serves as an exemplar of how to lose catastrophically.

Peter H. Wilson is Chichele Professor of the History of War at the University of Oxford and author of *Iron and Blood: A Military History of the German-Speaking Peoples Since 1500.*

The Lost Division at Stalingrad, by Iain MacGregor

The Battle of Stalingrad ended on the 2nd February 1943, 80 years ago. The author of an acclaimed new history tells us here about the German 71st Division under General von Hartmann that was almost entirely destroyed in that seismic clash between Nazi Germany and Soviet Russia.

President Vladimir Putin's decision to send his armed forces into the sovereign state of Ukraine on 24 February this year has caused Europe's largest refugee crisis. Almost a quarter of the Ukrainian population (9.8 million) have fled the fighting and key cities such as Mariupol, Kherson and Kharkiv lie in ruins with the historic port of Odessa and the capital Kiev under missile strikes. This conflict has seen an expected speedy Russian victory turn into a bloody war of attrition with Russian forces taking heavy losses as the nimbler western-backed Ukrainian militias and regular units make significant gains as we progress into the winter. Whether he believes it from his lackies, or not, Putin's dream of restoring the lands of old imperial Russia lies in tatters, alongside the prestige of his armed forces, now tarnished in the west for a generation.

As it was in the Cold War (1948-92) Soviet forces are once again seen as the sadistic and cruel aggressors, only this time magnified ten-fold by 24-hour news and smart phones which bring the horrors of the war to every one of us.

The relationship between this recent Russian history and its preeminent place as the heroic country that suffered catastrophic losses in the Second World War seem to many historians like me a million miles away. The cult of sacrifice is a strong one in Russia, stretching back decades through the Cold War and into the country's war with Nazi Germany once Adolf Hitler had launched his invasion of the old Soviet Union on 22 June 1941.

History's greatest conflict would ebb and flow, the losses mind boggling for both sides as Joseph Stalin became an ally to the western powers and 'Uncle Joe' was voted 'Man of the Year by *Time Magazine*. The German juggernaut looked unstoppable, until the winter of 1942 and Hitler's all-conquering armies were destroyed at a city in southern Russia, 15-miles long and lying like a ribbon along the banks of the country's greatest river – the Volga. The city names after Russia's famous dictator - Stalingrad.

There is a passion for the fight for Stalingrad. The industrial Soviet city sat on the edge of Asia is seen by many as the key European battle of the Second World War, the defining campaign when the momentum and invincibility of the German army was firmly halted. Strategically and psychologically, it was the turning point for the Red Army's fortunes that would end in their capture of Berlin in May 1945.

Operation *Barbarossa*, Adolf Hitler's initial grand offensive the previous summer to knock out Russia in a single campaign, had failed. Though suffering over 3 million casualties, the Red Army's counteroffensive outside the gates of Moscow had driven the Germans back and saved Joseph Stalin's capital. Weeks of subsequent bitter fighting in freezing conditions had left the Fuhrer stabilizing his own lines, though still deep inside European Russia and pondering his next move. Compounding his desire to strike a fresh decisive blow was Hitler's rash decision to side with Imperial Japan and declare war on the United States of America in December 1941. He realised what Germany would require maintaining its war machine indefinitely - oil.

Operation *Blue* would be Hitler's five-month-long offensive beginning on 28 June 1942 as Hitler's summer offensive struck south toward Russia's oil fields in the Caucasus. With more than 1.5 million troops, 3,000 armoured vehicles and over 1,500 aircraft it caught Stalin by surprise, who expected a repeat assault on Moscow. Blue's goals were ultimately to seize Caucasian oil and control its transportation along the river Volga. In June, Stalingrad, the modern industrial city named after the Soviet dictator that lay on its banks, was only a place on German commander's operational maps. It held no relevance.

However, as Operation Blue began to unravel due to Soviet resistance and Hitler's own disastrous oversight of his forces, it led him to fixate on capturing the city which bore his adversary's name. The battle would rage from early September to February 2, 1943. It would end with the annihilation of arguably the Wehrmacht's most experienced formation, the Sixth Army led by General Friedrich Paulus. This powerful force had been at the vanguard of the conquest of the Low Countries and France in 1940 and the initial invasion of Russia in June 1941.

General Paulus commanded over twenty-four battle-hardened divisions, a mixture of armour and infantry, supported by the Luftwaffe. He had smashed his way eastwards across several-hundred miles of barren countryside Russian's called the 'steppe', tackling fanatical Red Army resistance until his forces by early September looked upon Stalin's city, which stretched for fifteen miles, almost like a ribbon, along the western edges of the Volga. Stalingrad was a mixture of feudal wooden shacks in its south, modern boulevards, parks, and apartment blocks at its center, and three giant factories to its north which had switched from building pre-war farm equipment to becoming a vital center of Soviet tank production. For Hitler, capturing the city and eliminating its population of over 400,000 would inflict a phycological blow to the enemy and give him a platform for offensives the following summer. For these reasons, naturally, Joseph Stalin ordered the city to be defended to the last round. The battle would be the most ferocious of WWII.

At the heart of the fighting was a German formation whom I spent months researching, unearthing reports, diaries, letters and photographs. The 71st Infantry Division, commanded by Major General Alexander von Hartmann, like many others, would be destroyed in the fight for the city as it was ground down by relentless urban combat. A formation that comprised of three infantry regiments of three battalions apiece, supported by artillery and logistical units in support were the backbone of the German Wehrmacht. The 'Lucky Division' as it was called hailed from Lower Saxony in southern Germany and had won its spurs in the French campaign of 1940 before surviving its first year on the Eastern Front in 1941/42. Von Hartmann was a Prussian, a highly experienced and hard-nosed combat leader who had led a regiment in the French campaign and now been promoted to command a division. He carried his Great War (1914-18) service in the form of a limp from a severe leg wound suffered at the Battle of Verdun in 1916, but he drove his men hard and fairly and led by example.

As Germany forces surrounded the city along its length, Paulus reacted to Hitler's directive that Stalingrad should be taken quickly, the 71st Infantry Division would be in the vanguard to assault the city and attempt to capture its heart of the modern center. The Luftwaffe struck on 23 August, thousands of bomber sorties over the next few weeks focused on terrorizing the population, destroying key buildings, and dominating river traffic. Their destructive prowess however, played against German tactics of mobile warfare, which struggled to navigate a rubble-strewn landscape which now caused a stream of casualties in Paulus's infantry.

For his initial assault on the city itself on 13 September, the task to quickly capture the central districts, split in two the enemy's defences was allocated to three veteran units, one of which would be the 71st Infantry Division. It's supposed strength, however, was only on paper. A division that had been 15,000 -strong now comprised of some battalions no bigger than companies, made worse by a severe lack of experienced combat leaders and NCOs who had been killed or wounded in the campaign thus far. The assault would see bloody fighting for the capture of buildings and locations now famous in the Stalingrad story: the Railway Station No. 1, and the NKVD complex, the Central Ferry Crossing overlooking the Volga, and the highest point of the city, the enormous hill known as the 'Mamayev Kurgan'.

The first week of fighting would set the tone for what was to come. Intensive German artillery and aerial bombardments met with volleys of deadly Soviet Katyusha rocket salvoes to pave the way for infantry assaults and counterattacks (over 2.9 million shells would eventually land on the city). Then the infantry would close upon one another in a fight to the death for command of the city's key strategic points. The assault by the 71st Infantry Division that day would see German troops suddenly involved in hand-to-hand fighting for not only streets and buildings, but the floors and rooms within them and the sewers and cellars below them. This was a new style of intimate, primeval combat, fought with machine guns, grenades, flamethrowers, sharpened spades, and knives. Within a few weeks, cynical German troops would dub this 'Rattenkrieg' ('War of the Rats').

Von Hartmann's division enjoyed dramatic success early on due to the initiative displayed by one of his regimental commanders – Lieutenant Fritz Roske, who had addressed his officers prior to the battle:

'We stand in this phase of the struggle, which is of exceptional importance for the war and especially for the Eastern campaign. The whole world looks at the troops from Stalingrad and besides, the quick and victorious conclusion of the battle with the reaching of the Volga also means a conclusion for the regiment. The troops are to be informed of this. I expect the whole regiment to exert a great deal of strength, which will be worthy of the achievements of IR 194 so far.'

His troops followed him willingly into the maelstrom and by late afternoon had achieved their objectives, much to von Hartmann's jubilation at divisional headquarters. The Russian response to the catastrophic news that the enemy was now on the banks of their beloved Volga was immediate. General Chuikov ordered an immediate counterattack by reinforcements coming across the Volga.

As September gave way to October and the temperature dropped, the Germans pushed through the city relentlessly, with casualties mounting. Each time Paulus believed he had finally pushed his beleaguered enemy into the Volga, fresh reserves were rushed across the river by Chuikov in the nick of time to stave off defeat and stabilize the shrinking line. On 14 October, Hitler issued Operational Order No. 1 suspending all other operations along the entire Eastern Front, other than Stalingrad. The success of Case Blue now rested on the fight for the city.

By the end of October, the southern and central districts were almost all in German hands, with Chuikov's defenders holding on to slivers of territory. The 71st combat diary now celebrated its own local victory:

'At 1200 hours, the German national flag was hoisted over the Theatre and the Party building complex by the commanders of I.R. 211 and 191.'

This signaled to Hitler that the city was captured. He was wrong. The fighting would grow in intensity.

By mid-November, the temperature dropped yet further, bringing a stinging cold wind from the east as the waters of the Volga within a few weeks turned from slush to become floating, drifting ice. The Sixth Army's final drive to capture the last pockets stalled in exhaustion. Whilst Chuikov tactics were focusing Paulus in the city, miles into the frozen Russian steppe, fresh Soviet armies were massing undercover to strike a killer blow.

Operation Uranus began at 0720 hours on 19 November as the armies of General Georgy Zhukov struck to the north of Stalingrad. The following day, the Red Army attacked to the south. Within days both forces met 50 kilometers behind German lines at the strategic town of Kalach. Paulus's forces were now encircled with fresh Russian forces arriving to strengthen the new line. German attempts to relieve them by land and air were all doomed to fail as the conditions deteriorated and Russian military strength increased.

The remnants of von Hartmann's division were firmly ensconced in strong positions within the city, local troops knew it as 'Hartmannstadt.' The Axis perimeter that stretched for miles from the city was reduced over the following weeks by Soviet offensives until Paulus's troops fell back to the city. Outside von Hartmann's positions the Soviets had parked a truck with a large loudspeaker attached to its roof, broadcasting a clear but brutal message:

'Every seven seconds a German soldier is dying in Russia. Stalingrad is a mass grave.' The message was then enhanced by the sound of a clock ticking for seven seconds.

The remnants of the 71st Division now faced south and east, looking across the frozen Volga at a lunar, icy landscape that four months earlier had been a shining river and beautiful green forests.

The end game for the Kessel was fast approaching by 25 January. In the side streets could be heard the familiar rumble of T-34 tanks. Artillery and mortar shells intermittently dropped all around the German bunkers, foxholes and ruins. Casualties were increasing, with nowhere left to house or treat them. The lucky ones bled, froze, or starved to death in temporary field hospitals set up in bunkers or cellars. Hitler's order to defend Stalingrad to the last man, the last bullet, was more than carried out. Defeat was in sight.

The previous evening, over dim candlelight, von Hartmann had decided what needed to be done as he took a final drink with fellow senior commanders. His division had now been reduced to less than two hundred fighting men and a few artillery pieces, but he himself would not surrender:

'An officer has to die in battle. I shan't shoot myself, but I'll sell my skin for the highest possible price.'

Through the morning mist, German sentries lying in their foxholes squinted into the sun at the outline of five figures trudged towards them from the rear, seemingly oblivious to the thump of Russian mortar rounds landing in the distance. The first lieutenant on duty, crouched with his men in their positions in the snow, was astonished to now realize it was von Hartmann, accompanied by five senior officers with carbines slung over their shoulders as if it was just another day on their divisional shooting range back home in Lower Saxony.

Hartmann greeted his junior officer, who continued to lie prone on the ground, squinting his eyes to focus on his commander. The young officer gave him the situational report. The general thanked him and gestured that he remain lying on the ground. He then unslung his rifle. He stared across at the enemy positions. The Russians were becoming agitated at the movement in the German lines; activity could be seen in the Russian positions. The sound of more mortars rounds landing was heard behind the German forward positions as the morning peace was shattered. Shots suddenly zipped past von Hartmann's group, kicking up spurts of snow near his feet. He took up a shooting stance with his front foot perched on the snow hillock the officer lay behind, and chambered a round. His companions soon joined in the engagement.

Though eyewitnesses claim he did wound several of the enemy, a Soviet marksman managed to get into position and kill him instantly with a shot to the right temple. Von Hartmann's troops dragged their fallen commander's body back from the front line and buried him in a foxhole dug into the frozen earth of the railway embankment. As the news spread, many of the men admired the fact that their leader had taken an 'honest bullet.' Many other German officers would take such a route, too, rather than be captured.

The Sixth Army would surrender a few days later with Field Marshal Paulus (now promoted by Hitler in the knowledge that he needed to follow von Hartmann's fate) walking into captivity along with 90,000 Axis troops and so bringing an end to WWII's greatest battle. Only 5,000 men of those who trapsed across the wintry steppe that day would make it home in by the mid-1950s. The cream of the German Wehrmacht, including the 71st Division was laid to rest by the Volga; destroyed by their Fuhrer's hubris, the tenacity of the Red Army and the Russian winter.

Iain MacGregor is an acclaimed historian and the author of *Checkpoint Charlie: The Cold War, the Berlin Wall and the Most Dangerous Place on Earth.* His latest book is *The Lighthouse of Stalingrad: The Hidden Truth at the Centre of WWII's Greatest Battle.*

Why Colonialism? By Nigel Biggar

In a bestselling new book, the academic and ethicist Nigel Biggar has examined Britain's colonial past with a moral lense. He has done so with a nuanced and balanced approach, taking into account the negative, as well as positive aspects of empire. Here he explains his reasoning.

Colonialism: A Moral Reckoning contains a lot of history. If it does nothing else, I hope it will inform Britons, young and old, of the *whole* truth about our three-hundred-year career of imperial endeavour all over the world. For it tells not only of the tragic, lamentable and abhorrent elements, but also of the heroic, admirable, and humanitarian ones. It offers those who identify themselves as British cause, not only for shame, but also for pride.

So, readers will learn—if they really need to learn—about the 150 years of British involvement in slave-trading and slavery, justified by the racist belief that black Africans were naturally inferior.

But they will also be reminded that slavery was an ancient and universal institution, such that even slaves who escaped into the mountainous forests of Jamaica kept slaves of their own in the 1700s—as did freed slaves in the American south up until the eve of the civil war in 1860.

They will be reminded, too, that Britain was one of the earliest states in the history of the world to abolish the slave-trade and slavery within its territories, on the basis of a Christian and Enlightenment conviction of the basic equality of all human beings, regardless of race and relative cultural development.

Britain then used its imperial power for the next 150 years to suppress the slave-trade and slavery from Brazil, across Africa, as far as Malaysia. In the 1820s and 30s the slave trade department was the largest unit in Britain's foreign office. And in the mid-1800s the Royal Navy devoted 13% of its total manpower to stopping the Atlantic trade alone.

And, yes, readers will read about Britain's unjustified belligerency against the Qing Empire in the Opium Wars of the mid-1800s; about the bloody vengefulness of some British in suppressing the Indian Mutiny of 1857; and about the disproportionate use of force by General Dyer in 1919 when he kept his 50 Gurkha and Indian troops firing into what happened to be an unarmed crowd of 25,000 people in Amritsar for an unrelenting six to 15 minutes.

But they will also be reminded that the British Empire was at its most violent during the Second World War, when from May 1940 to June 1941 it offered the *only* military opposition—with the sole exception of Greece—to the massively murderous racist regime in Nazi Germany.

When Churchill decided to keep Britain and her empire at war with Germany after the fall of France in May 1940, he really did not do it for profit.

But *Colonialism: a Moral Reckoning* is not primarily about the past; it is about the present and the future. Or rather, it is about the past *only because* it is about the present and future.

Let me explain.

In May 2015 I published an article in the *Scottish Review*, offering a moral justification for Britain's nuclear deterrent. In response, early the following year Michael Fallon, then Secretary of State for Defence, invited me into the Ministry of Defence to talk about Scottish nationalism and Trident.

As I was taking my leave, Michael asked me what I was planning on doing next, and I replied that I was thinking of writing about the British Empire. I have no idea what Michael thought, because his face betrayed nothing. But I do remember thinking to myself, 'Oh my goodness, that must sound really eccentric'.

This was seven years ago, remember: long before the current 'decolonising' rash broke out.

But the connection was this. As an Anglo-Scot, I had had a unionist dog in the fight that was the 2014 referendum campaign on Scottish independence. During it, I had been struck by a remark by Jim Gallagher, one of the brains behind 'Better Together' movement, namely, that the nationalists had all the uplifting music, all the romance—whereas unionists seemed able only to talk in the monochrome, transactional terms of pounds and pence.

Ever since then, with due respect to Gordon Brown, I have been sceptical that further tinkering with constitutional structures would succeed in puncturing the demand for independence. That is because Scottish independence is a solution in dogged search of an adequate problem, a faith in dogmatic search of a rationale.

And that faith is generated by an exhilarating tale of a new-born Scotland cleansing itself of a clapped-out Britain, which has been discredited by its imperial abuse of hard power, and is embarrassing itself as it totters across the world stage like some sorry, faded actress (I paraphrase Tom Nairn).

The truth, however, is quite different. Britain today is generally wealthier, healthier, more secure, less class-conscious and less racist than it has ever been. It remains an important, if secondary, pillar of the liberal democratic West. And not many things would delight the West's totalitarian enemies in Moscow and Beijing more that to witness the disintegration of the UK. Recalling the final days of the referendum campaign in September 2014, the then British ambassador to the UN has written: "My Russian opposite number sympathised with barely suppressed glee at the prospect of the UK dismembered and its permanent seat on the security council called into question. It was clear to me that Scottish independence would have had a devastating impact on the UK's standing in the world, much greater than withdrawal from the EU ever would".

Therefore, it is vital to the cause of keeping the UK together, sustaining the West, and so diminishing the appetite for independence among Scots, that the more admirable truth about Britain's three hundred years of imperial engagement with the world be told. For only so will young, liberal, humanitarian Scots find the idea of Britain attractive, want to identify themselves with it, and think of themselves as British.

That is one way in which the story my book tells about Britain's imperial, colonial past is important for her present and our future—and for the present and future of the West in general.

Another is this.

In 1976 the Baghdad-born Jewish historian, Elie Kedourie, published his book, *the Anglo-Arab Labyrinth.* in this he wrote: "No doubt, great powers do commit great crimes, but a great power is not always and necessarily in the wrong; and the canker of imaginary guilt even the greatest power can ill withstand".

The guilt he had in mind was the conviction that the British had betrayed the Arabs in permitting Jewish immigration into Palestine after the First World War, since they had promised that Palestine would be part of a new Arab state.

Kedourie argues convincingly, I think, that Britain had in fact made no such promise and betrayed no one. Nevertheless, the canker of *imaginary* guilt had come to infect the British Foreign Office, to weaken British self-confidence, and to misshape British foreign policy.

Today, we are again succumbing to a fresh and more general guilt about our colonial past, which is determining the decisions and policies of our cultural institutions, weakening the soft international power of the Crown, and making us vulnerable to infinite claims of reparation for ancient wrongs.

(You should be aware that almost every one of the 15 chapters of Sir Hilary Beckles' 2013 book, *Britain's Black Debt*, takes care to open by quoting a member of a recent British Labour cabinet or shadow cabinet. Should Labour win the next general election, we can expect the demand for reparations to gain traction in government.)

By telling the whole truth about Britain's imperial past, the good as well as the bad, my book contradicts the false equation of British colonialism with slavery and racism, in order to cure the British of the canker of imaginary guilt at a time when the liberal West needs to keep all of its pillars standing.

In his 1942 novel, *The Man without Qualities*, Robert Musil mused on the decline of the Austro-Hungarian Empire on the eve of the First World War. He wrote: "However well founded an order may be, it always rests in part on a voluntary faith in it. Once this faith is used up, the collapse soon follows; epochs and empires crumble no differently from business concerns *when they lose their credit"*.

Colonialism: a Moral Reckoning aims to restore credit to Britain's past, in order to inspire faith in Britain's future. That is what it is really about.

Nigel Biggar is Emeritus Regius Professor of Moral and Pastoral Theology at Oxford University and the author of *Colonialism: A Moral Reckoning*. You can listen to an interview with Nigel and the Editor on the Aspects of History Podcast.

Pilgrim of Peace: Anthony Seldon Interview

In his latest book, Prime Ministerial biographer Anthony Seldon has traced the route of the Western Front in remembrance of a First World War officer who was killed in the conflict. Our editor met him to chat about the journey, and about Seldon's views of the Great War.

Despite more than 100 years passing since Armistice Day on the 11th November 1918, the First World War is still able to prompt emotions among many in Britain and France. So many families were impacted, with the British dead numbering approximately 750,000, and the wider Empire in total numbering 1.7million with France losing nearly 5% of its population. It's therefore no surprise why visitors to the Western Front make the journey every year. In 2021, Anthony Seldon made the pilgrimage, but in a slightly different way. He was seeking to walk the entire Front, from the Swiss border to the Belgian coast, around 1,000km away. Not only was he going to do this epic walk (at the age of 67), but he was doing so to create the Western Front Way and has documented his odyssey in a new book, *The Path of Peace*.

It's a book full of feeling, not least because the death of his wife from cancer in 2016, which obviously had a profound effect on him. His decision to embark on the walk was also inspired by the letters of Alexander Douglas Gillespie, a young Argyll & Sutherland Highlanders officer killed at the Battle of Loos in 1915, in which he expressed a desire to create a walking route along the Front. Mackenzie's dream has now been realised by Seldon, and in 2022 both cycling and walking trails were in operation to allow pilgrims to World War One to visit all or part of the allied front lines.

When I met Seldon, though, I was concerned for his physical well-being after he'd completed what is an impressive achievement, during much of which was done with excruciating blisters (requiring several hospital visits along the way). He confirms there are no lasting ill-effects, which is a relief, "Well, thank you for asking that. I just had a look and checked - they're still there." More importantly, though, why is it that on an emotional level we are more interested in the First World War than the Second?

"It's a great question that I, and many people…may have reflected about. The Second World War is fascinating. And of course, we have much better colour photography and we have moving film of the battles. We don't have any moving shots of the battles of Ypres and Passchendaele and the Somme, or Verdun. There wasn't the technology to do that at the time to capture moving battle scenes. In a way we have less idea about it, and yet somehow it seems to be nearer. I think it's got a lot to do with the sheer magnitude of the horror. The scale of losses, nearly a million people killed, and on the Battle of the Somme, 60,000 casualties on just the first day. The sense of the folly and the damage it did to communities across the whole country. Now, that's three times as many dying as in the Second World War, which lasted almost two years longer. A much more horrific war, and a war which might not have thrown up lots of great photography, moving images of battles, but it did throw up a great deal of poetry and remarkable writing and indeed, remarkable painting."

My own feeling about the First World War was originally influenced by row upon row of names of dead in my school chapel's crypt. Influenced too by Wilfred Owen and Siegfried Sassoon, and then of course, Blackadder, but that changed when discovering the deaths of my two great uncles, and the injuries to my own grandfather. If the war had been a waste, then had their sacrifice been wasted also? One of my great uncles, Ion Carter, had joined the British Army before the outbreak of the war. He was of an artistic disposition, and not particularly good with money. As a young officer, when a cheque he had issued bounced, he was discharged from the army, and cut off by his father. After the war began, he re-joined, but this time with a new name, Christopher Valentine, and from the ranks. He rose to the rank of Sergeant, winning a Military Medal along the way, but was killed at Arras in 1917. I've visited the CWGC site and his name is on the wall of the memorial, presumably because his body was not found. Was it worth it? After all, I got the impression from the book Seldon thinks not.

"The Second World War was far more obviously a war of good against evil, or good resisting evil coming from Germany and coming from fascism. The fundamentally racist ideology of nationalistic wars that were fought and the loss of 6 million Jews, but the loss of 50 million people together in that war, as opposed to…'only' 19 million in the First World War. Had Hitler not been resisted in the Second World War, then the whole of Europe could have fallen under that terrible regime that denied democracy, denied freedom, denied many of the liberties that we love as human beings...In the First World War, it was far less clear that the German regime or Austro-Hungarian, was in any way more brutal…or more anti-democratic than the regime in London. Yet you could also say that it was Germany that invaded Belgium, and had invaded northern France, and needed to be resisted. As against that, Germany was saying it was merely acting first before it was surrounded on both sides by enemies, bringing a great threat. So it's more of a morally complex issue.

"Did 1945…lead to peace in Europe undeniably? And Germany wasn't humiliated in the same way after the Second War as it was after the First, and neither were, to the same extent, other defeated powers…Peace has reigned, pretty much, for the last 75 years or more. Whereas after the First World War, within 19 years, Europe [nations] were back at each other's throats, having had very unstable years following the First World War. It is less evident the First World War was fought to secure a better world."

Given my own family's experience, and many others across Europe, the thought that the sacrifice had all been for nothing is not a happy one.

"I think this is where one needs to be careful. When I was coming back, as I described in the book, there was the scuttle out of Afghanistan and the very real sense then from the families of 454 British servicemen, as well as these far greater numbers of American families who had lost loved ones in Afghanistan. What was that all for? Clearly, the First World War was about a lot more enduring gain than the Afghanistan war had been. People like Siegried Sassoon questioned the validity and the need for the war, but it happened. People showed enormous courage, self-sacrifice, dignity, heroism and loyalty who took part in this war that was supposed to be the war that would end all wars…I think for somebody who lost relatives in the war, definitely it was fought for something, even if the moral absolutes are not as clear as in the Second World War."

Of course, Seldon is most well-known for his numerous biographies of British Prime Ministers, starting with John Major, with the Johnson biography due out this year. I'm unsure if Liz Truss will trouble his pen. For many of their predecessors, the First World War had a profound impact, either through their own service, or through their children.

"…It's very much a question for debate whether seeing suffering makes for more contemplative, cautious leaders who will go much further to avoid war, or whether exposure to blood and gore makes people more angry and vengeful. Putin has seen a lot of the horrors of war with his own eyes, but it's done nothing to make him a more compassionate or peace-loving leader. So I suppose the jury has to be out on that and you need to have horror to make you a more civilised, decent human being. Let's hope not. And yet you can't help feeling that Churchill was affected by his experience in the First World War and by what he heard about what happened at the Gallipoli, which he was in part responsible for. And it did make him more cautious about committing British troops in the Second World War, particularly into them going over the top in ways that would result in mass numbers of death.

"Andrew Bonar Law… lost children which was extraordinarily painful, and the Prime Minister, HH Asquith lost his son Raymond. And I talk in the book about how he went across to the Battle of the Somme to see Raymond and what a wonderful time they had, how that evening Asquith went to the headquarters…and was drinking with Haig and how Haig told his wife that he got altogether rather sozzled that evening. But at least he had gone across and seen the battle. You can see bits of that all the way up to present day with Johnson going to the Ukraine, obviously not British troops fighting, but to gain a closer sense understanding what's happening.

"In a way, it's perhaps a good thing that leaders do have their children fighting because it makes them more cautious about not committing other people's children to fight in avoidably dangerous positions. But equally, the effect on a leader is devastating, utterly devastating…It was hard for Asquith and Bonar Law to continue being as effective as leaders carrying that extraordinary grief of the loss of child. So again, a lot of these questions don't have direct answers, but they probe challenges and people can be found on both sides of these arguments."

The walk that Seldon has established, and which is now up and running is important so that future generations can keep the flame alive. And of course, if you're walking through Alsace, Lorraine, Champagne, northern France and Flanders, French and Belgian hospitality will ensure all participants are suitably refreshed throughout. Seldon's final words are resonant, however.

"This path is all about learning from and learning to embrace and ultimately, yes, to love people for their differences rather than to hate people. And the hatred leads to war. And on and on that cycle goes."

Sir Anthony Seldon is the author of a number of acclaimed Prime Ministerial biographies. He is also the author of *Path of Peace: Walking the Western Front* Way. You can listen to the extended interview with Anthony on the Aspects of History Podcast.

Short Story: Maker of Gold by Nick Brown

Panopolis, Egypt, 298 AD

In many ways, the day started well: I awoke from a restful, uninterrupted sleep; enjoyed a hearty breakfast of bread, cheese and dates with my wife; and was ready to depart by the second hour. But as I opened the front door, my mother-in-law darted out of the kitchen and gripped my arm. I knew what was coming.

'A dream, Zosimos.'

I tried not to show my displeasure. On the whole, I have no objection to my wife's mother; nor the practice of interpreting dreams. However, when one hears of such things on a weekly basis, one becomes rather less convinced of their significance. Her dreams often took the form of premonitions and I must admit that she had accurately predicted several events in the past. In recent times, however, few of her imaginings had materialised.

'Mother, I must go.'

'It was clear, so very clear. A man, clad in red.' She gazed up at me, green eyes unblinking.

'Is that all?'

'He will come to you.'

'And?'

'Whether he means ill or good, I cannot say.'

My house is situated only a short walk from the Temple of Min. I was glad I'd chosen my lighter tunic, for the day was a warm one; the sun clear and bright, the sky free of cloud. I had much planned for the next few days, and with the natural signs so favourable, my chances of success were good.

I can say without an excess of pride that I am a well-known person in my city, and as usual I exchanged greetings with many. The second half of my route took me along the Avenue of Septimius Severus. I heard the familiar cracks and thuds of the stone-cutters within their great yard and it was here that I saw a Christian man whose name I could not recall. We exchanged a nod, for our paths had crossed once or twice at social functions. He looked nervous; no surprise given the Emperor's attitude towards his people, which was increasingly echoed by my fellow Egyptians. I did not share such hostility, perhaps because I'd spent much of my life studying the works of fellow practitioners from various faiths.

As I turned off the avenue towards the temple, a caravan passed by: dozens of heavily-laden camels guided by weary riders. Judging by the amount of sand stuck to them, they were not long from the desert.

As always, I stopped at the one place on my route where I could see the bountiful Nile. Even this brief sight of the brilliant waters brought a smile to my face.

The Temple of Min is one of the greatest holy places in the whole of Egypt, and the largest building in my city. Min is a god of fertility, worshipped here for centuries. In the time before the Greeks, the city was Khent-Min, but to them the god was Pan, hence the change of name. The temple is painted blue, and almost every surface is decorated with images of gods and birds and animals. I passed through the chill shadows of the broad, high entrance, where craftsmen were etching a poem in the stone.

I did not intend to tarry long, for the priests tend to make considerable demands on my time. Many outsiders consider *me* a priest – for there are divine aspects to my work – but I consider myself an artisan, and my official title is *master craftsman*. I simply could not begin the day without praying to Min so I hurried to the central shrine and knelt before the granite statue. Realising that I had not brought a votive for some weeks, I resolved to do so on the following day.

Once out of the shrine, I proceeded towards the rear of the temple and the vast walled compound where myself and hundreds of others are employed. Within the temple itself are chambers for priests, administrators, librarians, healers, embalmers, musicians and astronomers. In the compound are the craftsmen: bakers, beekeepers, weavers, builders and metalsmiths such as myself.

Upon seeing High Priest Hermaios hurrying towards me, I struggled not to grimace, as I'd hoped to at least begin my day's work without interruption. Such is the life of a master craftsman.

'Master Zosimos, may the gods favour you this day.'

'May they favour you, High Priest Hermaios.'

With his tall frame, hairless head and spotless white robes, Hermaios cut a striking figure. I sometimes felt rather inferior in my drab grey tunic but I cannot say that the high priest and his compatriots treated me in such a way, for they grasped the practical realities of my work.

Hermaios spoke softly, as pious men often do. 'I mentioned you and your labours this morning in my prayers. I gave an offering to great and honoured Thoth, so that he too might aid your efforts.'

'My thanks.'

'There are three issues I must mention.'

Hermaios often employed this opening; I suppose it helped him remember.

'Of course,' said I, affecting a patient manner.

Around us, the compound was already busy, and I noted the weavers overseeing a delivery of freshly-cut rushes.

'The order for Gargonius,' said Hermaois. 'It will be ready for the end of the month?'

'Indeed, it will.' I had already given my superiors numerous assurances on this matter. Gargonius was a Roman merchant with a fleet of ships that ran between Panopolis and Alexandria. He had asked for a dozen small statues of the Roman gods to decorate his new villa. Though I cared more about my research than profit, it was important that my guild fulfilled such contracts. These earnings formed a significant part of the temple's revenue and funded my work.

'Good,' said Hermaios. 'And have you spoken to Mersis today?'

'No.'

'Please do. The astronomers report an unexpected change in the ninth constellation.'

This was not a significant concern for me. Over the years, I had concluded that the position of the sun and the moon were of more significance to the sacred art than the stars.

'Thank you for notifying me. The third matter?'

Hermaois sighed. 'Yesterday we were visited by Timon, representative of the Temple of Dendara. They are supporting Nelios and his new guild.'

Nelios was a fellow practitioner of the sacred art who I had known for several years. He'd originally joined me as an apprentice at the Temple of Min but, over time, acrimony had developed between us. Though initially eager to learn, the young man proved difficult to educate. While my efforts were based largely on the texts of those that came before me, Nelios was dismissive of such research and relied too much on haphazard experimentation.

He had left the temple two years ago to form his own guild. While not yet in a position to threaten mine, his boastful character and bold claims ensured that his was a name I often heard.

'Well,' said I, 'that is their problem.'

'I suppose so.' Hermaois paused, evidently choosing his next words carefully. 'But Timon expressed … disappointment at your criticism of Nelios. In these matters, your opinion is greatly respected.'

'Believe me, I would prefer not to ever mention the man. But his manner and methods are detrimental to the art. I do not ask other practitioners to follow me; I merely advise them not to follow *him*.'

Hermaois held up his hands to appease me. 'And there can be no doubting your knowledge in such matters. But relations between ourselves and the Temple of Dendera are currently good, which gives everyone in Panopolis a better chance of ensuring the continuance of our ways. The current governor seems to respect our traditions but there's no telling what may change in Rome.'

'Understood. If I am asked my opinion of Nelios, I will give it. Otherwise, I shall not mention him at all.'

'Very well.' The high priest placed his hand on my arm. 'Master Zosimos, please know that we are all fully aware how lucky we are to have you. I shall not keep you a moment longer.'

One of my five assistants was ill with a fever, and three had been temporarily seconded to the temple to assist with some painting. That left me with Kastor, the youngest but most enthusiastic of the five, and I felt confident we would still be able to achieve much.

My main workshop is large: thirty paces by twenty, with a dozen circular windows to provide plenty of light. The building is constructed of mud-brick, which resists fire well and provides a consistent temperature. I was pleased to find that Kastor had already started the furnace and added another layer to Gargonius' statues. I took one outside and held it up to the light. The apprentice had perhaps used a little too much oil in the mixture but I said nothing. Kastor had only been with me for a few months, and though he'd rather been foisted upon me (as the son of an eminent priest), I couldn't fault his efforts so far.

Before carrying out the main task of the day, the young man and I knelt upon a sunlit patch of floor. I instructed Kastor to conduct the invocation, in which we appealed to the gods, the daimons and the elements. Through this we sought to harmonize our bodies and minds with the natural and the divine.

Once the invocation was complete, I inspected a delivery of bronze, which had recently arrived from a new supplier. I intended to heat a sample and remove the surface layer of copper. Only then could I begin to understand the characteristics of this particular alloy.

While we waited for the furnace to reach the appropriate temperature, Kastor cleared his throat. 'Master Zosimos, might I ask a question?'

'Do I not always say that you should?'

'You do, sir.' The young man scratched his cheek, then nodded at the sheets of metal. 'We are producing what some call Corinthian bronze – that is bronze transformed into gold.'

'On this occasion, yes.'

'And you are educating us in the other methods of altering substances to create gold.'

'Indeed.'

'Yet we also work with *pure* gold – the metal mined from the earth.'

'And how can we tell what is gold?'

Kastor counted the five markers on his fingers. 'Extreme weight, yellow colour, shine, resistance to marking, resistance to fire.'

'Precisely. What you refer to as "pure gold" demonstrates these characteristics more robustly than Corinthian bronze, smelted orpiment or any of the other materials. But there is no reason not to consider them variations of gold. All are the gifts of the gods.'

From the temple came the familiar sound of drums and bells. I glanced down at my hands, now illuminated and warmed by a shaft of sunlight.

'We who study the sacred art are part of a great, ongoing endeavour. We could not work without those who came before us; and those who come after us will build on our achievements. That is why we must be rigorous with our observations and record-keeping. I believe there will come a time where men like us will develop the ability to create what is currently only given to us by the gods of the earth.'

I was pleased by the expression on the young man's face; and the fact that he'd noticed the furnace was in need of more fuel.

'Sir, shall I-'

'Please.'

I turned my attention to the bronze. When the furnace flared, I spied some spotting in the metal that looked like arsenic. Once Kastor had finished adding firewood, I called him over.

'There is a volume by Bolus of Mendes that includes a section on impurities I'd like to consult. I believe it's the eighth. Can you fetch a copy from the library?'

'Of course, Master.'

'Kastor, don't ask Librarian Eugenios – his eyesight is terrible.'

I was about to begin heating the sample of bronze when I heard footsteps behind me.

'That was quick,' said I, assuming it was Kastor. But upon turning around, I found myself face to face with a stranger.

The man was difficult to age. He looked to me like a desert tribesman, for he was clad in black robes, his face lined and worn. Despite his weathered features, there was not a trace of grey within his thick beard.

'You are Zosimos.'

He spoke in halting Latin, his mouth ugly with jagged, yellow teeth. I was relieved to see no trace of a weapon.

'Who are you?' said I.

'Do not matter.'

'You waited for Kastor to leave – until I was alone.'

'Yes. This temple busy.' As the tribesman walked forward, he put both hands up, as if ready to attack. My eyes were drawn to one of his long, baggy sleeves, for I thought I'd seen something move under the cloth.

'Why are you here?'

'Send message. You talk about others. Too much.'

I recalled my mother-in-law's warning. Here was a man clad in black instead of red, but his intentions were clearly not good. I could hardly believe that even Nelios was capable of such an outrage but surely he – or some ally – was behind this.

I backed across the workshop, between two tables. The stranger followed me. I have seen eyes like his before: soldiers, warriors, those for whom violence is nothing more than work.

'Need to keep quiet.'

Now I clearly saw his left sleeve bulge. There was something alive in there.

'You see her? My girl.'

The man reached into the sleeve with his right hand and brought out a small snake: eyes a hateful black, slender purple tongue scouring the air. It was close enough for me to see the individual scales of a burnished pale red.

'Spitting cobra,' said the tribesman. 'Won't kill. But will blind. Hard to work then, no?'

I continued my retreat, and now looked around for something to defend myself.

The stranger stretched out his arm. The snake's head bobbed from side to side, its cold gaze fixed on me.

'If I were you, I'd put that thing away.'

This calm yet authoritative voice spoke in immaculate Greek, with the accent of a distinguished Roman. Dragging my gaze from the cobra, I saw a tall man stride into my workshop. Behind him were two legionaries.

The tall man drew his sword, closely followed by the soldiers. The three polished blades gleamed orange from the light of the furnace.

'Quickly now,' said the Roman, 'or I'll have my men chop that thing's head off.'

The tribesman looked back at him.

'If I have to ask again, it won't be the snake's head.'

The tribesman returned the reptile to the recesses of his sleeve, then turned away from me and withdrew. Only now did I realise that he was a small man, his diminutive frame dwarfed by the three Romans.

'Escort our charming friend to the garrison,' ordered the tall man.

The defeated tribesman left my workshop with two blades aimed at his back.

I don't think I have ever been quite so grateful to see one of my mother-in-law's premonitions come to pass.

The interloper wore a red, long-sleeved tunic and a broad military belt with a buckle of lustrous silver. Having sheathed his blade, he walked across the workshop towards me. It was normally centurions that wore red but this man carried no helmet or armour.

'It seems I timed my visit well. Who was that?'

'I don't know his name. I believe he was sent by an enemy of mine.'

'Really? Well, give me the enemy's name and I'll do what I can to ensure he never troubles you again. You are Zosimos, the renowned maker of gold?'

'I am, sir.'

'That is a relief.' The Roman leant back against a table and folded his arms across his chest. 'I have spent the last week sailing up the Nile, the week before that crossing from the capital. I work for a man who works for the Emperor. Some idiotic governor in Pannonia has signed a peace treaty with a tribe of barbarians. We need the treaty to hold but he promised them a thousand pounds of gold and, well, I gather there's currently little to spare. I understand that you can produce something that looks genuine but is less expensive?'

I was only now beginning to recover from my scare and here was another odd turn of events.

'I must thank you for your intervention, sir, but you should know that I am very busy with my work for the temple.'

'Fear not; I will ensure the priests are properly compensated. But we do need this stuff quickly. I have chartered a ship and would like to get it back to Rome with all possible haste.'

My goodwill towards the interloper was fading. His request would involve a huge amount of organisation and work. Then again, if he really was in Panopolis on behalf of the Emperor, what choice did I have?

'I mean, we wouldn't want to disappoint the Emperor, would we?'

There was only one answer to that. 'No.'

The Roman wandered towards the furnace and tapped the sheet of bronze with a knuckle. 'I mean, between you and me, it doesn't have to be top quality.' He smiled. 'Just good enough to fool a barbarian.'

Nick Brown is a novelist of ancient Rome and the author of *Tarchon : Agent of Rome*.

How to Tackle a Mongol Invasion: Fight, Flee, Capitulate or Negotiate?
By Nicholas Morton

In this entertaining piece, handy advice is provided by the author of a new history of the Mongol horde. Should you run away or stand your ground?

In the early thirteenth century, societies across Eurasia confronted a common peril – Mongol invasion. As the century progressed, armies led by Chinggis Khan and his commanders won battle after battle, civilizations falling like a house of cards. In these years, the Mongols' conviction that they possessed a divine right to rule the entire planet looked unnervingly plausible.

This was a time of acute uncertainty for rulers and communities who still maintained their independence. How should they respond to the gathering storm? Their choices were fairly limited and the Mongols' ambassadors offered such peoples only two stark options: submission or invasion. This article will consider the effectiveness of the various policies adopted by leaders across the Near East when facing overthrow.

In this predicament some chose to resist and many Near Eastern powers sought to defend their frontiers. These included Sultan Kay Khusraw II, ruler of the Anatolian Seljuk sultanate (a powerful empire occupying much of central and eastern Anatolia – modern-day Turkey). He led his forces into battle against the Mongol invaders in 1243 and suffered an overwhelming defeat at the battle of Köse Dagh, following which the Mongols besieged and sacked many of Anatolia's major cities, forcing the Seljuks to submit to their hegemony.

Others sought to negotiate. Witnessing the overthrow of the powerful Seljuk Sultanate, the much smaller kingdom of Cilician Armenia in southern Anatolia took the decision to submit to the Mongols, even before the Mongols armies reached striking range of its borders. This was a pragmatic choice. Cilician Armenia's small army had no chance of defeating a major Mongol field army.

There was a strong vein of logic to submitting quickly to the Mongols. Historically, the business of conquering countries by force has always been a risky undertaking and even the most able commanders will lose many troops in the process. It is therefore much more desirable for conquerors to convince countries to submit via diplomacy without having to fight long and expensive campaigns. Following this reasoning, the Armenians almost certainly knew that by submitting early to the Mongols they would be very leniently treated by their new masters because the Mongols would want to encourage other civilizations to follow their example. This proved to be the case and the Mongols' tribute demands on Cilician Armenia were not nearly as damaging as the heavy payments required of other civilizations. Later, working within the Mongol system, the Armenians managed to secure a relatively preferential status for themselves, enabling them to win further concessions for their people in later years.

Submission or invasion may have been the two options proffered by the Mongols' envoys and yet a third option was to try and 'string-out' the diplomacy, neither submitting nor refusing to submit. This approach seems to have been taken by the Byzantine Empire of Nicaea who managed to prevaricate on the issue of submission for many years; their strategy seeming to be: to keep the Mongols talking and thereby stave-off either capitulation or invasion. This was naturally a risky approach. The was a danger that the Mongols would ultimately become frustrated and force the issue by despatching an army of conquest. Nevertheless, the Byzantines played a very careful diplomatic game and they had the geographical advantage that their small empire lay a long way from the Mongols' centres of power. On one very memorable occasion in 1257 Mongol ambassadors arrived on the Byzantine border only to be guided by their hosts along the most meandering route imaginable in order to reach the capital city of Nicaea. The intention was to give the Mongol deputation the false idea that the Byzantine empire was vast, requiring a journey of many days to traverse. This impression was only amplified by the deployment of large numbers of troops at every stage of the journey, the goal being to suggest that the Byzantines possessed enormous military resources. In the event however, the arrival of new Mongol forces in the Near East a few years later drove the Byzantines to the negotiating table and they too reached an accommodation with the Mongol Empire.

A final option was simply to try and evade the Mongols, by relocating to safer territory, further from their advancing forces. Many people - whether individuals, families, communities or societies – selected this option, especially nomadic societies, which were inherently more mobile. In particular many Turkmen communities moved either into Syria or western Anatolia, seeking refuge from the Mongols. Some went on to found small powerful beyliks of their own in Anatolia while others attached themselves to existing powers. This approach had the advantage of enabling these communities to evade the Mongols' armies, but naturally much depended on their ability to build a new home for themselves – whether by force or negotiation – in a new landscape.

Reviewing these hard options, none of them guaranteed success or security; they all entailed major risks. Still there is a pattern here that warrants attention. It is conspicuous that the societies which fared best were often those who made extreme choices. For example, the Armenians didn't submit when threatened by immediate invasion, they submitted much earlier and benefitted from this choice. Had they waited until the last possible moment to submit then the Mongols would almost certainly have been far harsher in their demands.

Another example of extreme behaviour being rewarded can be seen in 1260 when a huge Mongol army advanced into Syria, conquering Aleppo and Damascus. Faced with this new threat, the Mamluk Empire of Egypt responded by adopting a position of the utmost pugnacity. Rather than awaiting a Mongol invasion across the Sinai Desert into Egypt, the Mamluks actually marched out against the Mongols, advancing beyond their borders to seek combat. They made no attempt to keep open a diplomatic channel with the Mongols, choosing instead to kill the Mongol ambassadors who reached their court. No other Near Eastern power had adopted so extreme and aggressive a stance towards the Mongols previously; most had been far more cautious and waited behind their borders for the Mongols to make the first move.

In the event, the Mamluks' choices led to a significant victory over the Mongols at the battle of Ayn Jalut in 1260. Admittedly this came about in part because events played out in the Mamluks' favour. Shortly before the battle, the bulk of the Mongol army withdrew to the east, seemingly on hearing news of the death of the Great Khan in Mongolia. This meant that the Mamluks with around 12,000 troops encountered a Mongol garrison of a roughly similar size, rather than the full Mongol army of over 100,000 troops. Nevertheless, this should not diminish the importance of their adopted strategy. Previously, scarcely anyone had ever sought to actually invade Mongol territory, newly conquered or not. The Mamluks' bold decision to do so effectively wrong-footed their opponents and this goes some way to explaining their success.

Of course, both the Mamluks' and the Cilician Armenians' policies contained inherent perils and these became apparent particularly in the long-term. The Mamluk victory over the Mongols at Ayn Jalut was not decisive; it took over sixty years of war to eventually fight the Mongols to standstill. The Mongols could not ignore the Mamluks' victories; their thought-world centred on the belief that they had a right to rule the world and so defiance could not be tolerated. To this end, the Mamluks needed to wage campaign after campaign before securing a peace agreement in 1323. As for the Armenians, their decision to submit early guaranteed their survival only while the Mongol Empire itself remained strong. During the later thirteenth century, however, the Mongol Empire became riven with civil war, splitting up into rival territories (the Mongol territories in the Near East becoming known as the Ilkhanate).

In this new era of infighting, rebellions broke out across Mongol territory, especially in Anatolia and the once powerful Mongol Empire proved increasingly unable to protect satellite states, such as Cilician Armenia.

Reviewing the differing choices made by these societies provides much food for thought. We live an age today where cautious, well-planned, proportionate, and incremental policies are generally deemed to be the safest and most prudent courses of action. In an age of conquest, however, this is not necessarily the case. The Armenians survived not because they submitted to the Mongols at the point of the sword, but because they submitted at such an early juncture. The Mamluks survived not because they chose to resist the Mongols, but because they went one stage further and actually sought to make war against them. In both cases their very different, yet extreme, policies paid dividends.

Nicholas Morton is an Associate Professor at Nottingham Trent University. The author and editor of many books, his most recent publication is *The Mongol Storm: Making and Breaking Empires in the Medieval Near East.*

AoH Book Club: Saul David on Zulu - The Heroism & Tragedy of the Anglo-Zulu War.

Saul David's *Zulu* was widely acclaimed when it was published in 2004. With such rich subject-matter it's no surprise, but coming after *The Indian Mutiny* and *The Homicidal Earl,* the title cemented David's place as the historian of the 19th century. Our editor met up with him recently to discuss the history of the Anglo-Zul War.

Saul, this book deals with the Anglo-Zulu War of 1879, but what was the state of play in Southern Africa at the time?

You have to go back to understand the British connection to southern Africa, to 1806, when the British arrived in the Cape Colony, and their first move was to muscle out the Boers, who'd been there from a couple of centuries earlier, and the Boers gradually moved to the north. This had a knock-on effect to a lot of the African tribes and nations that they were going to bump up against. Slowly but surely, the Brits expanded their footprint in southern Africa to include the Natal Colony in 1843. So you've now got two Crown Colonies, you've got two Boer republics, the Orange Free State and the Transvaal, and you've got a number of quite powerful African kingdoms, one of which is Zululand. Now, Zululand is far and away the most powerful African kingdom of that time.

At one stage, it encompassed 250,000 Africans and it had been created by conquest towards the end of the 18th century. The Zulu tribe was really very small. It was only about 1500 strong. You can see that partly down to the military genius of the Zulu king Shaka, and the revolutionary means of warfare that he introduced. You had this massive expansion of Zulu land, not only subsuming tribes that it had conquered, but also influencing a lot of tribes further afield. So the actual spread of the Zulu kingdom was probably twice as far as its actual territorial borders. Now, if you move on to the late 1870s, you've got a situation where the British are getting more interested in confederating southern Africa. Now, the reason they want to do that, interestingly enough, is not because they are interested in expanding the empire per se. They want to make the empire more affordable. They want it to be self-supporting. So they want to create a system down there where the white settlers really are going to get some form of self-rule, which, of course, has just been given to Canada and will eventually be given to Australia and New Zealand.

Looking through your book again, this Zulu culture is highly militaristic. It's reminiscent of ancient Sparta, which I wonder is maybe one of the reasons why the British were quite fascinated by the Zulus in the Victorian period?

It is indeed. In fact, they were known as the Black Spartans. And you're right, the analogy is a very good one. There's also another analogy, which is that their tactics were very similar to the tactics the Romans used. So there's this extraordinary link with ancient warfare, and yet there is absolutely no evidence that they ever understood or ever knew anything about Greek warfare, or indeed Roman warfare. The young boys in Spartan culture were brought up to be warriors. They were famously sent out when they were very young and forced to live in really tough conditions. For the Zulu boys, it was very similar. They were taken away from their families at a very young age and effectively put into mini-regiments. When they came of age, they would join the regiments proper, and the society was incredibly militarised. The young men in Zululand could not marry without permission, and once they married, they would then move on to a separate married regiment. So it was all incredibly ordered and wives were chosen for them.

The great Zulu victory is at Isandlwana. Do you mind talking about the battle?

The British move is pretty aggressive. There's an invasion of Zululand on three axes. Three forces invade and it's the central one that we're most interested in, because that was the biggest one, the Central Column, as it was known. It crossed at Rorke's Drift into Zululand and its intention was to bring the Zulus to battle. There was an assumption among the commander, Lord Chelmsford, who hugely underestimated the power of the Zulus, that they wouldn't fight and therefore he would have to find them and bring them to the battle. Now, this is a complete misunderstanding of Zulu culture and Zulu battle tactics, which are incredibly aggressive. They've developed this short, stabbing spear that can only be used at close quarters. The whole system of their battlefield tactic is to close with the enemy, surround the enemy and then fight at close quarters. Chelmsford has hopelessly misunderstood what's likely to happen and of course, as a result, is not taking as much care on the line of march as he should have done, because he's thinking, "I've got to find the Zulus" whereas in actual fact, they're coming towards him.

He goes in with an army of 5000 strong. He fatally weakens it by dividing it not once but twice, so that by the morning of the 22 January 1879, the camp at Islandlwana, which is the base, is just one of the camps along the way – they are heading towards the Zulu capital of Ulundi. The camp at Isandlwana is left with just 1700 men and only about 900 of those are British soldiers. The rest are African militia levies. It's a strong force, but it's not impregnable, as they're going to discover. And it is up against an army, as it turns out, of 20,000 disciplined, veteran Zulu warriors.

And Isandlwana is a perfect example of the famous tactic?

The horns of the buffalo, as it was known. They advance the main body or the chest of the buffalo, so you have a series of regiments that are assigned to the chest part of the formation, and their job is to fix the enemy. In other words, to engage the enemy and keep it fixed in a steady position. Meanwhile, the two horns of the buffalo go out on either side and they fully envelop the enemy, so they go all the way around the side. Now, again, this goes back to ancient warfare because it's the Battle of Cannae, basically. This is Carthage, this is Hannibal against the Romans in ancient times.

I suppose maybe we're just talking about kind of universal principles of warfare here and maybe we shouldn't be that surprised, but, yes, the battle was a perfect example of that. It didn't go as simply, of course, as the Zulus would have wished it to, because in the course of fixing the camp, that is the main body of the defenders in one position, they took enormous casualties - thousands of casualties, because, of course, those breach loading weapons were incredibly effective. But while that battle was going on at the front of the camp, these two horns were racing rounds at the back of the camp. And, of course, when they finally meet and they've trapped any retreat from the camp. Some do get out, but most are trapped. Then it's just a fight to the death. And as the afternoon wears on, the butchery continues until not a single living soul is left. That is about 1300 corpses and they've been killed with sharp edged weapons. So you can imagine it was a pretty gruesome sight.

We can't mention the war without mentioning Rorke's Drift and the film starring Stanley Baker and Michael Caine. The battle takes place on the same day, doesn't it? You've got the British outnumbered, being attacked, but this time they are in a secure position and there is certainly not a slaughter. I guess it is a victory, but it's one of the great battles in 19th century history.

It's certainly known as one of the iconic battles. The question is, was it ever as significant as was made out? My belief it wasn't. That's not to belittle the courage of the people who fought that battle. They were, as Lord Wolesley puts it, and Wolesley comes out shortly after these battles to take command from Chelmsford, "they were caught like rats in a trap and they fought, as you would expect people to do in that situation."

It was an extraordinary battle and it was fought because the bit of the Zulu army that had missed out on the plunder and the killing at Isandlwana, the reserve. It's been given orders to go to Rorke's Drift, but not actually to attack the Drift itself, because the Drift is in Natal, and that would have been seen to be a very aggressive act.

Cetschwayo, the Zulu king, had given his commanders orders not to cross the Tugela River and attack the Drift, but just to check it out as a show of force. Well, they disobey those orders mainly because they want a bit of glory. They also see the Drift, which is effectively a supply depot defended by just 100 soldiers and another 39 guys in hospital, as a soft touch.

The initial instinct of the two officers there, Chard and Bromhead, is to leave. In fact, an order is given to put the wounded in the wagons and they're going to set off. But luckily for them, they're dissuaded from doing it by Commissary, who's a senior NCO type figure called James Dalton, who says, "Well, I wouldn't recommend that, sir, because if we do that, the Zulus are very fast moving, they'll catch us on the way to the next town and we'll all be butchered. So we've got more chance of surviving if we stay here." So the decision is taken to create a mini-fortress out of the two main buildings at the Drift, which is the hospital and the main building, and fortify them with mealy bags and wagons and various other things. If you've seen the film *Zulu*, you'll know exactly what it looks like. It's a really accurate depiction of what they did there and how they tried to defend that position.

The battle begins as evening is falling on the afternoon of the 22nd, and it goes on all the way through the night to the early hours of the 23rd. During that time, there is wave after wave of attacks against the outer perimeter. At one stage, the Zulus break into the hospital, which, of course, is one of the keystones of the perimeter. They then have to withdraw to what they've called an inner perimeter, which has all been pre-planned in advance. Not by Chard, who takes the credit for all of this, but actually by Dalton, who's made all these suggestions as to how to construct the defence. Dalton is an ex-engineer, so he had the understanding, and they managed to hold out against attack after attack. It is incredibly dramatic. And again, the film *Zulu* is very accurate on this, until finally in the morning, the Zulus have had enough and they withdraw.

The nature of empire is that you inevitably have conflicts such as this where a larger aggressor is keen to take over a perceived threat. But what's interesting in this is that the British Empire, the government, didn't want the invasion to happen - and it's cooked up by one general and one colonial administrator.

The imperial government were no shrinking violets themselves. They very much understood the power politics at play in southern Africa. They wanted eventually to create a confederation of southern Africa. They hoped to do it bloodlessly, but of course probably realised that certainly in the case of the Zulus, a war would have to be fought. So it was really a timing issue, rather than the fact that they were against fighting that war per se. The ultimate aim is not to create a bigger British Empire, it is eventually to create a white-run, white-ruled political system that is Southern Africa or South Africa as it became, as a client of Britain's. We would keep our naval bases and our strategic relevance to that part of the world, too. It was pretty cynical what they were trying to do, but the idea that they were trying to expand the empire per se, no, that's a misunderstanding, if anyone ever imagines that is the case.

And in fact, most of the expansion of the empire in the 19th century is not a deliberate intention by the home government to expand the empire, because, frankly, most people felt that empire was expensive, which indeed it was, it had to be policed. And very few places in the empire actually produced money for the home country, as opposed to money going the other way.

Saul David is a historian and author of *Zulu: The Heroism & Tragedy of the Zulu War 1879* which is highly recommended. His latest book is *Devil Dogs*. You can listen to an extended interview with Saul on the Aspects of History Podcast.

Survival of the Fittest: The Pastons & the Wars of the Roses? By Anne O'Brien

In her latest novel, the sequel to The Royal Game, Anne O'Brien continues the story of the prominent Paston family, made famous by their letters. Here she describes their involvement in that brutal civil war.

What did the middling sort of people do, those who had an eye to climbing the social ladder, when faced with the tragedy of civil war? For many it was a matter of keeping their heads down, to emerge at the end in as much of one piece as was possible. If they were unfortunate, their manors would become part of the battleground, fought across and laid waste. If luck was with them, the fighting would pass them by, even in another part of the country, and they would emerge relatively unscathed. Whatever happened in the battles, it was good policy to do all that they could to keep in the King's good books, or under the beneficial eye of the local magnate. Survival was everything.

The Paston family found it very difficult to achieve either of these two options. To their benefit, their manors, mostly in Norfolk and Suffolk, were never in the path of marauding armies. Pure luck of course. But attracting the good offices of King or magnate was another matter altogether. The Paston menfolk certainly petitioned Edward IV for the security of Caister Castle and protection for the Paston manors from men such as the Duke of Suffolk and the Duke of Norfolk, with recompense for past attacks, but their success was limited. King Edward was not prepared to push for recompense when the support of the Dukes was far more important to him than that of Sir John II Paston.

As for the Dukes of Norfolk and Suffolk, in their relationship with the Pastons they were a law unto themselves. With a weak King such as Henry VI and a troubled King Edward IV with his own difficulties when facing the demands of Warwick and Clarence, the local magnates were given the freedom to follow their own interests. The Pastons became pawns in the local power-games. No one was prepared to stop the Duke of Norfolk from taking possession of Caister Castle, the jewel in the Paston crown. John III Paston might hold out in a short siege but the outcome was inevitable. The Pastons lost their castle. Getting it back would need a miracle.

As for the fighting. John I Paston managed to keep out of any battles, focusing on disputes in the courts of law. His sons were not so fortunate. John II and John III found themselves caught up in the net of bloodthirsty politics. Their greatest need was for a patron powerful enough to offset the local authority of the Duke of Norfolk. They found one in the Earl of Oxford. This put the Paston brothers in a good position, but it took them into war. When the battle lines were drawn the Earl called on the Paston brothers John II and III to fight under his standard and they could hardly refuse, even though it meant their taking a stand against the King when Oxford joined Warwick's rebellion. Thus, the Pastons both fought in the Battle of Barnet in 1471. Unfortunately, they ended up on the losing side when King Edward emerged victorious, Warwick was killed, the Earl of Oxford fled abroad and John III was wounded by an arrow in the elbow.

John III recovered, but the two Paston brothers had risked and might lose all. They were declared traitor by King Edward, with the likelihood of their possessions being confiscated. As was their uncle William Paston whose own royal connections were complicated by his Beaufort wife, daughter of Edmund Beaufort, Duke of Somerset, the Beauforts being distinctly out of favour at this time. Their defeat at Barnet might mean that all the Paston efforts to solidify their estates had gone for nothing. An anxious wait developed to see what would happen even though John II was 'betrothed' to Mistress Anne Haute, cousin of the Queen. They were fortunate that a royal pardon was offered, Edward IV needing all the friends he could get. Their estates were restored, but the ever-lingering problem of Caister Castle was not solved.

It has to be said however that the Pastons were not without a wily plan, on or off the battle field. How to get Caister back without a battle and with a patron who was in exile? The death of the Duke of Norfolk presented a fortunate opportunity. The widowed Duchess of Norfolk was brought to bed of her second child at Framlingham Castle. John III who had held a position in the Norfolk household in his youth, attempted to persuade his mother Margaret to visit the Duchess and offer her services during the birth, Margaret having survived seven births. It was John III's plan that his mother persuade the ailing Duchess to give Caister back.

Whether Margaret actually attended this event is unclear. She may have done so. If so, did the two women discuss such business dealings while the Duchess was in labour? I doubt it. The Duchess gave birth to a son who died almost immediately, leaving a young daughter as the heir to the Norfolk acres. Whether these two intrepid women had any effect on the fate of Caister, in May of that year the Royal Council at last pronounced in favour of the Pastons and the Duchess renounced it. Caister Castle belonged to Sir John II Paston and its ownership was never again questioned. It is encouraging to think that the work of women might have had an effect rather than warfare.

The Pastons were, it seemed, not always reluctant to pick up arms if it might play to their advantage. In early 1475 all five of the Paston brothers, sons of John I Paston, enlisted to fight under King Edward in the continual manoeuvring between England, France and Burgundy. England and Burgundy were in alliance against France and it seemed that war would ensue. In fact, war was averted and the Paston brothers returned home without shedding any blood, either French or their own. At least they had proclaimed their loyalty to the King.

During the final years of English unrest, the Pastons found it politic to keep their heads down. There was no direct Paston involvement in the Buckingham rebellion or the events that led to the death of Richard III and the crowning of King Henry VII. John III kept a discreetly low profile, keeping clear of all conspiracies. John was presented with three dangerous possibilities: to fight for his old patron the Earl of Oxford on one side, to fight for the Duke of Norfolk on the other side, or to sit tight and do neither. John wisely chose to sit tight and await the outcome. Ultimately however John III emerged from his political isolation to fight alongside the Earl of Oxford in the Battle of Stoke which put an end to the Lambert Simnel rising in 1487. As a reward for his conspicuous support John III was created Sir John Paston and Deputy Lord High Admiral. Their future was secure with the Tudors.

It is worth taking a final look at the fate of Elizabeth Paston, sister of John I Paston. She did not fare so well, her involvement in the Wars of the Roses being far more deadly. Her first husband Sir Robert Poynings survived involvement in Cade's rebellion, before they were wed, but then after their marriage he fought in the Battle of St Albans for the House of York. He was killed on the battlefield, leaving his young son as heir and his estates in difficulty for Elizabeth, since they were claimed by his niece Eleanor through the complications of Kentish patterns of inheritance. Since this troublesome niece was wed to the Percy Earl of Northumberland, she had far more influence than Elizabeth Paston. Elizabeth had to fight to keep the Poynings estates for their son Edward who should inherit, a struggle for possession that dogged her for the rest of her life.

Nor did her second husband bring any light relief for her. This was Sir George Browne who survived the battle of Tewkesbury on the side of the Yorkists but then became involved with the Kentish rebels in the Buckingham Rising against Richard III in the first year of his reign. Browne was captured when the rebellion failed, tried for treason as one of the leaders of the rebellion in Kent, and was executed on Tower Hill, leaving the Browne estates also in jeopardy. Elizabeth's Poynings son Edward also joined the rebels and was forced to flee, joining the exiled Tudor in his bid for the throne. Some women had much to suffer in wartime, but to Elizabeth's ultimate satisfaction Edward returned to England to become a notable member of the Court of King Henry VII. Her son with Sir George Browne was also restored to his estates with the coming of the Tudors.

The Pastons were not one of the major 'mover and shaker' families in the Wars of the Roses, drawn as they were into the fighting against their wishes. They were men of law rather than men of the sword, but they emerged in good order. Their value to historians is of course their comment in their letters. We are given a splendid bird's eye view of how these middling families survived and managed to turn events to their own interests.

Anne O'Brien is a Sunday Times bestselling author. Her latest novel *is A Marriage of Fortune*.

The Reel War: Military History & Film, by Tom Petch

How many times have you watched a war film and despaired of its accuracy? Historian and filmmaker Tom Petch sympathises with you, but there are some good examples out there.

War Films provide drama, tension and horror in the right quantities to keep audiences in their seats. Having been in both the military and the film industry I've seen first-hand the pressure on a film's historical accuracy of film production. The demands of getting the cast and equipment in the frame, and money on the screen, mean events which would be physically spread out, as real units and men would disperse for protection, are bunched up. Similarly, time scales have to be compressed – raids and battles that took hours or days become minutes, with several actions often combined for the narrative. Sound is distorted; the reverberations in the cinema floor or through your home Dolby speakers in no way resemble gunfire or shells, and characters on film are archetypes – if actors walked and talked like their real-life counterparts we would quickly tune out. But, while all this is understandable, directors, writers and producers often play fast and loose with the facts. As a friend and military film advisor recently complained; 'I don't know why they do it… For the same money they could get the real thing.'

Sir David Lean's fabulous portrayal of Peter O'Toole as Lawrence leading the charge on Aqaba in *Lawrence of Arabia* (1962) never happened. Aqaba was taken without a shot. The real Lawrence deceived the Turks he was heading north towards Damascus with a diversionary raid, and, after they had sent their cavalry after him, turned south to take Aqaba. After a short siege the Turks surrendered. In the only charge in that campaign Lawrence shot his camel in the head by mistake and somersaulted over its head. Characters get similar treatment. In a famous scene in *A Bridge Too Far* (1977) Robert Redford crosses a river under heavy enemy fire, but the real Major Julian Cook was not in the boat that day. The truth doesn't get in the way of a good story, as characters get credit for things they didn't do, and far more nuanced military operations are glossed over in favour of the type of action an audience expects when they pay to watch a war movie.

There are some notable examples that go the other way. The TV series *Band of Brothers* (2001), based on Stephen E. Ambrose's book of the same name, follows 'Easy' Company of 506th Regiment, 101st Airborne Division, and remains religiously true to Ambrose's research and veterans' transcripts and is the better for it. And, counter-intuitively, films that dispense with the facts altogether often manage to portray the truth. *The Battle of Algiers* (1966) and *Platoon* (1986) are fictional, but the better for creative input from veterans – Jean Martin in *The Battle of Algiers*, and Oliver Stone in *Platoon*. Martin plays French paratrooper, Colonel Mathieu, tasked with destroying the Algerian insurgency. When he gives a speech to his troops in the film describing his service with the French Resistance and in the Indochina War he isn't making it up. He did both. And the film's portrayal of how the French lose to that insurgency is so accurate it should have been compulsory viewing for all officers on the recent NATO deployment to Afghanistan. Stone, a successful screenwriter, had served in Vietnam and wanted to portray the reality of fighting the Vietnam War through the eyes of a small, albeit fictional, unit. It's impossible to argue that he didn't succeed. And on the subject of Vietnam, the overblown budget and scale of *Apocalypse Now* (1979), fiction based on the Conrad novel the *Heart of Darkness*, set in the 19th century Congo jungle, goes further than any to show the insanity of US involvement in Vietnam.

My own specialist subject is the creation of the SAS, and recently I've had my ear bent by veterans about BBC's *SAS Rogue Heroes* (2022) plot, portrayal of Sir David Stirling, and most recently the portrayal of Blair Paddy Mayne – so the question is, does the truth matter? After the carnage of the First World War, officer-turned-military-theorist

Basil Liddell Hart pointed out that war is a part time profession – no commander or politician has ever fought a battle before and therefore it cannot be learnt by experience. He cited Bismarck in the opening line of his book on the subject: 'Fools say that they learn by experience. I prefer to profit from others' experience.' He went on to study campaigns from Roman to the First World War, and came to the conclusion that victory went to those who dared to use The Indirect Approach – the title of his book, which influenced modern war from its publication to the modern era.

But what then, if the portrayal of history is wrong? Putin is no fool, and thought he could knock out Ukraine in a swift military strike. Nor was Tony Blair, when he committed British Forces to Helmand, Afghanistan. Nor Donald Rumsfeld, with his desire for regime change in Iraq. All these men thought a war was going to solve their problem. Why? My answer is because they were raised on fiction. Most politicians have neither gone to war nor stood on a battlefield. The only place they can get that information is from portrayals of history in books, television and film. And while there's an argument that fictional portrayal of wars is good because it raises interest in the subject, and encourages the audience to look into real events, that is not true for children. Perhaps the most avid consumers of war fiction are boys. I first saw *A Bridge Too Far* at Leicester Square Odeon aged 11 and assumed this was an entirely accurate portrayal of events. Why would adults make this up? I found it terrifying, and, to be fair to Richard Attenborough, whilst the film may have inaccuracies, the theme that *Operation Market Garden* was hopeless is an accurate summary of events.

But too often war films glorify war. Military action is 'kinetic', heroes die bravely, and the film concludes the sacrifice is worth it. To quote First World War poet, Wilfred Owen, who was killed 6 days before the end of that war: 'My friend, you would not tell with such high zest, to children ardent for some desperate glory, the old Lie: *Dulce et decorum est, pro patria mori.*' So while we can portray war as fiction, we must also tell our children the truth. Or we may consign many of them to the body bags of our own generation.

Tom Petch is a former member of the SAS, the director of *The Patrol,* and author of *Speed Aggression Surprise: The Untold Secret Origins of the SAS*. You can listen to an interview with Tom on the Aspects of History Podcast.

Kush: The End of the World, by Simon Turney

In his latest novel Bellatrix, bestselling author has taken the Romans south of Egypt to the wondrous kingdom of Kush.

In the Legion XXII books (*Capsarius* and *Bellatrix*) our intrepid Romans come up against the warrior queen of Kush, but who was she, who were her people, and why did this conflict occur? Well, without wanting to drop a plethora of spoilers for the books, here's a precis.

Egypt was an ancient kingdom even when Rome was but a budding village on a hill. When the emperor Hadrian visited in AD 130, his wife and entourage were tourists there just like any modern visitor, wowed by the ancient sights, and she even left graffiti on the Colossi of Memnon. But Egypt had not survived for more than three millennia before Hadrian without their challenges. Like any empire, they faced opponents beyond their borders, including the Persians, who conquered the land in the 6th century BC, and then the Macedonians, who took Egypt in 332 BC, founding a dynasty of rulers that would end with Cleopatra VII after three centuries BC. And even before this, they had warred with (and been invaded by) the Hyksos people of the Nile delta a thousand years earlier. Their neighbours to the south, though, in what is now Sudan, were the Kushites.

The Kingdom of Kush was a relatively young land compared with Egypt, though still far more venerable than Rome, having arisen in the mid-3rd millennium BC. The culture blossomed on the great eastward curve of the Nile just north of Khartoum, with a capital at Meroe and a major religious cult centre at Napata. Though these people were distinct and different from their northern neighbours, they shared many traits with the Egyptians. Their culture grew in the dry deserts of North Africa, their world relying upon the annual inundation of the Nile. Naturally they absorbed much from their neighbours, building pyramids of their own, adopting dress with a number of similarities and even acquiring the Egyptian gods to the extent that they claimed the birthplace of the great god Amun at their own Napata.

But they were not Egyptian. Kush remained a truly separate kingdom until the 8th century BC when they actually invaded Egypt, setting Kushite kings on the Egyptian throne for a century, before they were once more ejected. From that time on, there was ever something of a rivalry between these abutting Nile lands, the border region strengthening and weakening, wavering repeatedly throughout Ptolemaic rule in Egypt. Then came the end of Rome's republic, the fall of Antony and Cleopatra, and Augustus's easy annexation of Egypt. It seems that upon gaining control of the 'Black Land,' Rome came to an agreement with Kush, which at this point controlled most of the territory south of the First Cataract, including the bulk of what is now Lake Nasser, formerly a critical region of fortresses. Peace. Albeit briefly.

The kings and queens of Kush differed from their Egyptian counterparts in at least one particular and important way. In Egypt, the Pharaoh was master of the land, and the queens were his consorts, with a reasonable amount of power, but always less than their male counterpart. The patriarchal nature of Egypt meant that throughout most of its history, until the late Ptolemaic era, when queens found themselves in sole control they had to assume a masculine role (witness the great queen Hatshepsut portrayed in statuary with the fake beard of the pharaohs.) Even in Ptolemaic Egypt, though the queens could be individually powerful, even the famous Cleopatra VII only achieved real recognition of authority when married to her brother as King. Things were a little different in Kush. Royal lineage in Kush passed through the female line, and so while a king would rule, if he died, his sister would often rule as a regent queen until her child was of age. These were the Kandake. The earliest such known queen was one

Shanakdakhete. By 25 BC, when my story begins, King Teriteqas is dead and the Kandake Amanirenas, although she has a son named Akinidad, rules alone, a fact confirmed by the reference to her as 'qore and kandake', translating as something like 'ruler and queen', or even 'king and queen'. Amanirenas is not the first Kushite queen to rule alone, and not the only powerful or famous one. She is, however, remembered by history (via the Roman geographer Strabo) as a one-eyed warrior queen. The image this conjures is not one of a feminine and passive character, is it?

In 25 BC, events transpired to give Kush an opportunity they had not seen in centuries. Ptolemaic Egypt had been powerful and secure, and Kush could not realistically turn a war-eye north. Furthermore, in the first years of Roman control of Egypt, the place was valued, strengthened, and made home to two legions. In 25 BC, however, the Roman governor of Egypt made a critical error. Aelius Gallus took the bulk of his forces and made a valiant, if short-sighted, attempt to annexe the lands of Arabia. His campaign was doomed, not least through trusting a local guide who led them straight into disaster. Rome could recover from such problems, of course. Crassus had lost legions against the Parthians at Carrhae, after all, yet Rome had endured and prospered and tried again. The survivors limped back to Egypt, licking their wounds, Gallus was recalled for his failures, and was replaced by Petronius as Prefect of Egypt. Things could be rebuilt and strengthened. Arabia had been costly, but not critical.

Kush had not been idle, though, in the absence of most of the Roman might. Apart from a few paltry garrisons, the bulk of Egypt's military had been dragged away to Arabia and suddenly, for the first time in centuries, Kush's rich northern neighbour was poorly defended. The Kandake Amanirenas spotted the weakness and gathered her armies, marching north across the disputed borderlands. We can only guess as to Amanirenas's plans. It seems unlikely in truth that she saw the opportunity to retake control of Egypt as they had done a few centuries earlier. Rome was a stronger proposition than the Ptolemies, and her reputation preceded her. The Kandake may, however, have pulled a little trick observed recently in the work a fairly unpopular world leader. She may have thought that Rome was suffering sufficient troubles that she could annexe the south, up to and including the First Cataract, and keep hold of it without reprisal. Certainly, her armies reached Aswan (ancient Syene) and sacked the Roman installations there. She may have thought she could add all the lands south of there to her own domain. Or she may have known that Rome would attempt to regain control and simply have planned on utter destruction and the theft of anything of remote value. She installed a garrison there, at Elephantine Island, and withdrew her force south with booty and slaves.

This is the world into which my characters emerge. The Kandake of Kush is a fearsome opponent, with a powerful army. She has taken treasures, and we know this for fact, given the bronze head of Augustus that was found at Meroe in Sudan, looted probably from Aswan in 25 BC, which is now the pride of the British Museum. That magnificent head would not be alone. Kush would have ravaged the lands they took, carrying away gold, weapons, statues and more, as well as sufficient slaves to seriously boost the Kushite economy. We are treated to somewhat sparse accounts of the campaigns that followed, which I will not detail for fear of ruining my books for new readers, but I will leave you with an image of the Kandake Amanirenas that, for me, sums up the fearsome queen of Kush and her armies, and the danger into which Rome marched: The one remaining confirmed portrait of Amanirenas, found at Barwa in Sudan, shows not only the fierce queen with a sword in each hand, an image powerful in its martialness, but shows us what she did with her captives. In a scene more powerful and gruesome than any Egyptian Pharaoh might commission, Amanirenas is shown seemingly hammering down with her sword hilt on a pile of captives, which are being eaten by her pet lion, images later also applied to the Kushite Prince Arikankharer.

Rome never extended her border beyond the First Cataract. I think I know why.

Simon Turney is a bestselling novelist and author of *Bellatrix*, sequel to *Capsarius*.

Historical Heroes: Charles Dickens, by J.C.Briggs

It would be hard to better this issue's Historical Hero, the great Charles Dickens. He's also the hero of J.C.Briggs' series of novels and here she tells us why.

From pasting labels onto pots at the blacking factory, from taking supper with his family in the Marshalsea Prison, to the top of the Victorian literary tree, Charles Dickens's story is a remarkable one.

The blacking factory by Hungerford Stairs, 'a crazy, tumble-down old house… overrun with rats' haunted Dickens, who remembered his servitude there as his soul's agony. It was twenty-five years before he visited the site again, and the experience no doubt accounts for the ferocious energy and ambition which drove him on to write first his Sketches by Boz, then his fifteen novels, his short stories, and the hundreds of articles for his journals, Household Words and All the Year Round. He found time to travel, to act with his amateur players, to make speeches, chair committees, and to write thousands of letters – there are fourteen thousand letters in the Pilgrim edition, and more keep turning up.

Everyone knows the name Charles Dickens as well as they know William Shakespeare. Everybody knows Pickwick, Fagin, Oliver Twist, the Artful Dodger, Little Nell, Quilp, Scrooge, Tiny Tim, Mr Micawber, David Copperfield, Uriah Heep, Miss Havisham – these are just a handful of the characters spun from his magician's pen. He was an amateur conjuror, too – he could magic a Christmas pudding from a top hat. It is his invention which I admire. The names alone give insight into his genius. He must be the greatest namer in all literature and many of them have entered the dictionary. We all know what it means to be a 'scrooge'; the word 'Pickwickian' was in the dictionary by 1840. Mrs Gamp's umbrella sprang from the page into common usage. Mr Gradgrind, the schoolmaster is perfectly named as is his fellow pedagogue, Squeers – he of the one eye when 'the popular prejudice runs in favour of two.' There are humorous villains like Chevy Slyme, and monstrous ones like Murdstone and Headstone, Murdstone, in his way the murderer of his wife; Headstone, consumed with jealousy and planning murder. Neither is a caricature, all surface, an accusation made frequently against Dickens. Murdstone is a psychologically acute study of cruelty as an exercise of power, and Bradley Headstone a psychologically true portrait of a man possessed to the point of madness, goaded by a sense of class inferiority to his rival and sexual jealousy. One has only to think of Iago. Dolge Orlick, too – what a name – is entirely convincing in his rage against the favoured boy, Pip.

Dickens is a maker of words and there are some gems in his works. 'Comfoozled' is used by Sam Weller in Pickwick Papers to describe Mr Winkle's lovelorn state – bamboozled and confused. He is probably flummoxed, too, a word which Mr Tony Weller maintains is Italian. Dickens is probably the first novelist to use it in 1837, the year of the publication of Pickwick Papers. It became more common by the end of the century. Not Italian, of course, but from 'flummock', a dialect word meaning a clumsy person. The word first appeared in an 1834 book called Delicious Chatter where it appears as 'flummix'd'.

In Nicholas Nickleby, a Mr Pyke threatens to 'smifligate' an old man who is in his way. Dickens seems to have appropriated the word 'spifflicate' which means to annihilate, perhaps adding the implication of smothering and stifling – a 'fanciful formation', says the OED. It would be on Dickens's part. No other use of 'smifligate' has been found. The singular 'Connubialities' appears in Nicholas Nickleby – meaning marital tiffs.

In Sketches by Boz, Mr Malderton is a little 'spoffish' man, as is Mr Percy Noakes. These are the only two uses of the word in Dickens. It's another dialect word, meaning bustling, fussy, officious. Another source tells me that 'spoffish' is derived from 'spoffle' – to look busily engaged over matters of little importance. Stephen Fry maintained that he invented the word, and it was appropriated to mean a cover or guard for microphones, but Dickens was there first. Whether Dickens made it up or heard it, we don't know, but it's absolutely the right word for Messrs Malderton and Noakes, busying themselves about other people's business.

'It was the best of times; it was the worst of times…' Who can forget the opening of A Tale of Two Cities? The 'season of Light… the season of Darkness… the spring of hope… the winter of despair', and later all England and France unrolling in a series of images of poverty, corruption, and cruelty as if in the camera's eye. Dickens is a poet, too. The magic I wrote of earlier is in his language. Dickens casts spells in the repetitions, the antitheses, the sentences without verbs, the images dissolving on the page, light and shadow alternating, the fog in Bleak House rolling among the shipping, 'creeping', 'hovering', 'drooping', the gas 'looming through the fog' with 'a haggard and unwilling look.' Inanimate things leap into being in Dickens. The world is full of realities which take on a dream-like aspect. Nothing is what it ought to be.

In the fog-misted Court of Chancery, 'dusty warrants have grimly writhed' under 'the unwholesome hand' of Jarndyce and Jarndyce. The Court is a nightmare place, which 'has its worn-out lunatic in every madhouse and its dead in every churchyard.' Elsewhere, a pulpit sweats, fires shrink in fear, or spring up as if to speak, a grim clock tells grim time. A clock might tell Lawyer Tulkinghorn, 'Don't go home', but it doesn't. In Great Expectations, Pip receives that warning and spends a restless night in a hotel room in which 'the closet whispered, the fireplace sighed' and the very walls have eyes. 'Mouldy sighs' breathe out in ancient rooms, leaves are 'tearful and shivering' in a storm. The teeth of church bells 'chatter' in the frozen air. Houses skulk in yards, an oyster might speak to the Emperor of China, and floorboards cry out, 'Stop thief!' to the trembling Pip.

From Dickens's inexhaustible imagination unlike things fly together to reveal the very essence of a character. Rapacious Mr Vholes removes his gloves 'like a man skinning his own hands'; the deceitful bridegroom, Lammles, wrings the neck of a bottle to drink its blood; David Copperfield is 'a tender young cork' between the corkscrewing Heep and his mother. Heep's clammy hand leaves tracks 'like a snail.' Mrs Waterbrook in black velvet is like 'Hamlet's aunt' at a party where the guests are 'ices for the occasion like wine', though Traddles finds himself seated in 'the glare of a red velvet lady.' Mr Merdle, a man significant only for his wealth is 'put out in his hall like a rushlight' – the weakest and cheapest of lights, and his hand is as cold as a 'fish slice.' Secretive Mr Tulkinghorn is 'an oyster of the old school, whom nobody can open.' Sir Leicester Deadlock is 'a coin of the conjuror's trick.' A black ox 'with a clerical air' stares accusingly at guilty Pip with stolen food in his pocket. Dickens is a great humorist, too.

And London, for which Walter Bagehot says Dickens is 'a special correspondent for posterity', is the real and unreal city in Dickens's imagination. London Bridge, the Tower, the river, the wharves, the shipping, the warehouses, the dusty churches, and the great mansions are all present. The mud in the streets is ankle-deep, no doubt thickened by horse manure and a million tramping feet, but surely only Dickens could have imagined the Megalosaurus waddling up the street, the first dinosaur in English Literature. The slums are all too real. 'On Duty with Inspector Field', an essay in Household Words, takes the reader from the criminal haunts of the rookery of St Giles's to the greasy dens of Whitechapel, packed close with men 'in various conditions of dirt and raggedness.' Men, women, and children 'for the most part naked, heaped on the floor.' There's a terrible comedy in the image which compares this heap of humanity to 'maggots in a cheese.' There's horror on the steps which 'shine with eyes' and in the 'spectral figure rising, unshrouded, from a grave of rags.' And nightmare in the river, 'creeping, black and silent' where the dead lie, 'a million fathoms deep'. Or, above, a dream of 'stars in unimaginable millions, glittering… from eternal space.'

Tom All Alone's in Bleak House is 'a villainous street, undrained, unventilated, deep in black mud and corrupt water… and reeking with such smells and sights…' It is surrounded by a warren of equally squalid streets and alleys. There is a nightmare quality in Tom All Alone's, too. A crowd watches a half dead form carried by, hovering about Inspector Bucket and Mr Snagsby 'like a dream of horrible faces.' Dickens packs in more. It is not just that he wants to show us the horror of the slums. There is social commentary for such ruin, poverty and disease have consequences:

'… there is not one obscenity or degradation about him (the unknown Tom), not an ignorance, not a wickedness, not a brutality of his committing, but shall work its retribution, through every order of society, up to the proudest of the proud…'

His journalism, his speeches, his letters to the newspapers, his charity work all testify to his concern for the poor and dispossessed, the marginalised and the forgotten. What was needed first, he argued was sanitation. Children brought up in filth and poverty would be 'stunted and perverted'. He championed education for the thousands of 'ignorant and neglected children'. The lack of schools, he said, was 'a mighty crime and disgrace'. Westminster was a 'dust heap'; in Little Dorrit, Dickens invents 'the Circumlocution Office' to illustrate the delays, the confusions, the labyrinthine hopelessness of government to do anything to alleviate the misery of the poor.

It was estimated that thirty thousand children were abandoned in London in the mid nineteenth century. Dickens distils them all into one boy in whom a faint light of hope glimmers. Jo, the ragged crossing sweeper, knows nothing, only that 'He wos very good to me.' And there he is, sweeping the steps of the foul graveyard where Nemo is buried.

Dickens has lasted. He is always about. Tiny Tim and Scrooge appear at Christmas. He's on television; letters turn up and cheques; objects he owned appear at auctions – dog collars inkwells, walking sticks. He's in the newspapers. The fact that he didn't go to Australia apparently led to the first England cricket tour of Australia; a headline in the Sunday Times declared that reading Dickens is better for mental health than a self-help book. New biographies emerge. Films are made. Critical studies come out; talks are given on and off-line. The Dickens Fellowship endures. Authors appropriate him – guilty. Too many to count, but Barbara Kingsolver's, Demon Copperfield springs to mind as a wholly convincing David Copperfield for modern times.

Dickens is a genius, flawed of course, containing dark matter. Carlyle perceived 'the dark, fateful silent elements, tragical to look upon.' Sociable yet solitary, compassionate yet capable of cruelty, sensitive and hard, genial and inflexible, quarrelsome and kind. His friends loved him, though he fell out with Mark Lemon, one of his closest companions, and with Thackeray, both rows over his separation from his wife – the darkest blot on his reputation. There are others, no doubt, but when he died, John Forster, his lifelong friend, wrote that 'nothing in the future can, to me, ever again be as it was.'

Tolstoy said, 'All his characters are my personal friends.' He thought Dickens the greatest novelist of the nineteenth century. Dostoyevsky admired his works; as did Van Gogh who wrote, 'By Jove, what an artist. There's no one to match him.'

Open any of his books and in you go to Dickens's world, full of things rich and strange, tragic and comic, magic turns of phrase and startling images. Sometimes mocked for his sentimentality or for creaking plots, yet unsurpassed as a novelist in his invention and unforgettable characters.

J.C.Briggs is the author of the Charles Dickens Mysteries, the latest of which is *The Jaggard Case.*

The Slipperiness of History, by Deborah Swift

The author of a trilogy of Renaissance set novels describes her heroine, the creator of a mysterious potion. Or was she?

I was really interested to read recently that the coded letters of Mary Queen of Scots have been deciphered by modern computer scientists and decoders. Undoubtedly this will give us hitherto unknown insights into what we know about her and her life. Historians and historical fiction authors may need to change their views depending on the new evidence.

A similar thing happened to me when I was writing the last book in the trilogy about Giulia Tofana, a woman who was renowned for inventing the poison *Aqua Tofana*, and was supposed to have poisoned 600 men in Renaissance Italy. I had already uncovered through my research that Giulia Tofana was probably an amalgam of three women, and not the single entity of legend.

Three women, not one

The mother, Theofania d'Adamo was executed for the crime of poison on 12 June 1633, but her daughter, Giulia (known as Tofana) survived. The third person in this triumvirate of poisonous women was Giulia's daughter, known as Girolama Spara. Until recently very little was known about the daughter so as historical novelists do, I fictionalised her birth, assuming she was a blood daughter of Giulia Tofana and her (also unknown) husband surnamed Spara.

About half way through writing the third novel in the series, from the point of view of the daughter, new evidence arose about the women in Giulia Tofana's family. In an old library archive in Italy, an American academic had unearthed the real-time transcript of the murder trial of Giulia Tofana's daughter, Girolama Spara, (also known as Gironima Spara) and published it. The document was originally kept under lock and key by the Pope at Rome's Castel Sant'Angelo, and from there ended up in the State Archive where it lay uncatalogued and undiscovered for generations. You can find the document translated by Monson at the end of this article.

History evolves

Of course I trawled through the new information, discovering with growing concern that my fictional view of events differed widely from this new evidence. I was shocked to discover that Girolama Spara was a step-daughter, not a blood daughter at all, and that Giulia Tofana had been married twice.

The ledger was in a poor state of repair, but Professor Craig A Monson had painstakingly resurrected it and translated it into modern English. The truth is less glamorous than the plot I had in mind for these characters, so what should I do? The past is both fixed and mutable. The two previous books were fixed, already out on shelves and readers were enjoying the story. The new information meant that I would need to be open to bending, or changing, the third book.

Would readers care? There are many schools of thought on this – on how accurate historical fiction should be, and it is debated endlessly by historians and novelists. From my point of view, I was obligated to finish the story I had set up with the characters remaining consistent within the series, yet also to incorporate the new information. The rules I set for that world needed to remain in place so that the reader feels they are in a real and secure locale, no matter where the story went.

Whatever character I create can never be the real person. Anne Boleyn has had hundreds of interpretations of her character. The events I describe can never be 'true', just as contemporary witnesses to any crime will have different views. A novel can't be 'accurate', just as someone trying to depict my life of yesterday could never be accurate, even with all the iPhone technology and photography available now, and if my diaries were in front of them, because life is too complex to render completely. What I hope to achieve in my novels is a tantalising whisper of what it might have been like to inhabit another era.

History continues to fascinate

It is exciting that at last we know more about the actual trial and details of the life of Girolama. She is nicknamed Mia in my book, because having a similar name to her mother Giulia, she was often confused with her, and this led to many errors of attribution. Many of the crimes assigned to Giulia actually belonged to Girolama and vice-versa.

I used maps, academic articles and transcripts of primary sources to complete the book, as well as the translation of the trial documents by Professor Monson, and I like to include historical notes at the end of my books to make it clear where (for the moment) the historical evidence is pointing.

Is The Fortune Keeper a true re-telling of Girolama Spara's life? Definitely not. Will it take you on a journey into the heart of a young woman in Renaissance Venice? I hope so.

Deborah Swift is a novelist and the author of *The Fortune Keeper*, the latest of her Renaissance series.

The Age of Distillery, by Mike Rendell

In a new history of gin, the historian Mike Rendell has revealed a disturbing past, brilliantly depicted by Hogarth. In this article, he describes the distilling boom that took off in the 19th century, alongside Britain's expanding empire.

Researching the history of gin throws up some interesting characters associated with the distilling process, perhaps none more so than Felix Booth, whose name is associated with arctic exploration. He had been born in Clerkenwell London in 1780, dying 69 years later in Brighton.

He was born into a family of brewers and distillers who had launched Booth's Gin in around 1740. It became famous for its hexagonal-shaped bottles with a red lion on the label, representing the Booth family crest. As a drink it became well-known as 'a gentleman's gin' and centuries later was the reputedly the favourite gin of both Queen Elizabeth II and the Queen Mother.

Felix Booth developed the business, which had originated at Clerkenwell, by opening a second gin distillery at Brentford, together with a brewery on adjacent land. Subsequently he opened another distillery, in Edinburgh. By the 1820s he could claim to be the largest distillery owner in Great Britain. Success brought considerable wealth, as well as status, and in 1828 he was made sheriff of London.

The circumstances in which he developed an interest in locating and exploring the fabled North-West Passage is unclear. The idea of a passageway linking the North Atlantic to the Pacific Ocean, potentially saving weeks if not months on trading ventures to the Far East, had long been a target for explorers.

What is clear is that the Royal Navy had commissioned an expedition, led by Sir John Ross, onboard the *Isabella,* supported by a smaller vessel, the *Alexander*, commanded by William Perry. In 1818, those two ships sailed to Greenland and crossed the Arctic Circle. Having explored Baffin's Bay the ships entered Lancaster Sound, with the *Isabella* some nine miles in the lead. Confronted by appalling visibility, Ross claimed that when the fog briefly rolled back he could clearly see that there was no way out of the inlet. He maintained that all further progress was blocked by a range of mountains, which he called Croker's Mountains, in honour of the First Lord of the Admiralty. So, he turned around, went back to where Perry was sailing the *Alexander* and in effect, said 'Time to go home.'

The problem was that Perry never saw the Croker's Mountains, and was convinced that Ross had thrown in the towel too soon. When the explorers returned to England, Perry wasted no time in explaining to his superiors that Ross had chickened out of his mission. To the chagrin of Ross, Perry convinced the Admiralty that he, Perry, should lead a follow-up voyage. Off he went in 1819, and sure enough, found no sign of the Croker range of mountains. He returned, very much the flavour of the moment, to a hero's welcome, leaving the reputation of Ross in absolute tatters. In vain, Ross begged to be allowed to have the chance to lead another mission, but the Admiralty was having none of it. He had embarrassed the navy; he had made the Admiralty a laughing stock; he was a coward.

Ross turned to Felix Booth and persuaded him to finance a private expedition. This involved forking out £2,500 to buy a second-hand paddle steamer, previously engaged to carry mail between Liverpool and the Isle of Man. The steamer, known as *Victory*, thereby became the first steam-powered ship to search for the North West Passage.

In all, Booth contributed £17,000 to the cost of the voyage, with Ross topping this up with a further £3,000. Off Ross sailed on *Victory* in 1828 on a voyage which was to take over five years. Ross made slow progress as he inched westwards – often having to hoist sails rather than use the steam-driven paddles. On 6 August 1829, he entered Lancaster Sound, the scene of his previous humiliation, and then disappeared from view for four long years. Winter after winter his ship was iced-in and exploration was painfully slow. New features, inlets and harbours were named after his sponsor, giving rise to 'Felix Boothia Peninsula' and 'Felix Harbour' along with 'Cape Felix', 'Gulf of Boothia' and the 'Isthmus of Boothia' – and many of these names still appear on modern maps.

Remarkably, Ross managed to maintain discipline onboard the ice-locked vessel, ensuring that the crew kept fit with regular exercise. He also came up with innovative ideas to combat boredom, introducing literacy classes, and lessons in mathematics. In 1831, he sent his nephew James Clark Ross on an overland trip due north, hoping to find an open passage of water. Nothing was found, but on 1 June 1831, James Clark Ross became the first European to reach the magnetic North Pole. He constructed a cairn, claimed the land in the name of the British Crown, and headed back to tell his uncle.

That year *Victory* only managed to sail eleven miles in the entire year, before succumbing once more to an ice-bound winter. Provisions were dropping to a dangerously low level, signs of scurvy were evident in the crew, and the sled dogs were dying of starvation. The decision was made to abandon *Victory* and to half-sail, half-drag the lifeboats back to where they came from. It was an extraordinary feat of hardship and perseverance, and was met by a suitably extraordinary piece of good fortune: they were rescued by the *Isabella*, the ship on which Ross had sailed fourteen years earlier. This time around he may have failed to locate the North-West Passage but had managed to map an area of over half a million square miles, significantly narrowing down the search area for subsequent explorers.

Ross returned to Kingston upon Hull in October 1833, his reputation fully restored. He was presented to King William IV, he was knighted and greeted by cheering crowds wherever he went. And the restoration of his good name was entirely down to the encouragement and generosity of one man – Felix Booth, who was, in turn, made a baronet in recognition of his generosity. As 'Sir Felix Booth' he became a founding Fellow of the Royal Geographical Society and in 1834 was elected a Fellow of the Royal Society. William IV also granted the gin his royal seal of approval in 1833, resulting in its subsequent nick-name as 'the king of gins'.

It was small wonder that when Ross went back to the Arctic in 1850 as an old man – he was seventy-two – he named the ship on which he sailed *Felix*. Ross died in London in 1856 and is buried in Kensal Green Cemetery having outlived his sponsor by six years.

Sadly for Sir Felix, his philanthropy was not always so appreciated. One of the people he tried to help was his godson, born to his second cousin, and who was also called Felix Booth. Young Felix was born in 1805 and seems to have felt that life owed him a living. He asked Sir Felix for a job, and was given a position working in the distillery. He was not best suited to the position, given that his only skill lay in drinking the profits. He was sacked, but then asked Sir Felix for different employment. He was given a position looking after the poultry on a farm owned by Sir Felix. This involved free board and lodging along with profits from the poultry business but this was insufficient to satisfy the ungrateful godson. He then decided that he wanted to run a shop, and held out the begging bowl. Again, Sir Felix came up with the money, only to find that a year later his godson wanted more money for stock. Sir Felix declined, because his godson was unable or unwilling to produce any accounts showing where the earlier money had gone.

It left one very ungrateful young man determined to cause the maximum amount of damage to his elder relative. Aware that Sir Felix seemed to be offering financial help to someone employed by him as a confidential secretary, Felix tried to blackmail Sir Felix, alleging that Sir Felix was having a homosexual affair. Sir Felix declined to pay up; the allegation was made public and Sir Felix was forced to face a very painful allegation of something which was not just a criminal offence, but one which carried the death penalty. The young Felix was charged with blackmail, and sought to justify the allegation by 'naming and shaming' the recipient of Sir Felix's largesse. The man in question was John Marshall Marr, a former soldier then in his thirties (at a time when Sir Felix was in his early sixties). It totally backfired when Sir Felix publicly acknowledged that Mr Marr was his natural son, the result of an affair with a Scottish woman some three decades earlier. He was simply doing what any father would do in the circumstances, giving his son a decent start in life. Young Felix was found guilty of blackmail, sentenced to twenty years transportation to Australia, and disappeared from public view. Newspapers, particularly in the North of England, were awash with the story. Poor Sir Felix – he never deserved the humiliation and pain caused by somebody he had bank-rolled.

Sir Felix died very suddenly, of heart failure, in January 1850. He was unmarried, and the baronetcy passed to his nephew J Williamson Booth. In his will Sir Felix made financial provision for his illegitimate son, who married, moved to Exeter, and had eight daughters and four sons. The gin business which Sir Felix had headed continued to be family-owned for most of the nineteenth century until the death of Sir Charles Booth (nephew of Sir Felix) in 1897. The business was sold to the Distillers Company – forerunner of Diageo – in 1937. Throughout the 21st Century the gin was only sold in the United States. Production ceased in 2017 when the name was sold to the Sazerac Company, and they started to sell 'Booths Finest Old Gin' in 2022 - and it follows an old Booth tradition of being matured in oak barrels formerly used for sherry production.

Mike Rendell is a writer and historian and author of *A Dark History of Gin.*

Short Story: Ladies and Gentlemen, by Carolyn Kirby

Victorian London

Heads turn as we enter the foyer. Our gowns are shimmering in the chandelier dazzle; mine scarlet and white, Margie's emerald and black. The women's eyes that slide our way are envious. The men's eyes, trained on our figures, are hungry.

'Sister,' I squeeze Margie's elbow a little tighter, 'they are all looking.'

She does not reply. But the flutter at the corner of her mouth and the press of her arm on mine, tells me that she also feels a leap of excitement. At last, we have a recompense for our costly and sometimes painful efforts to make a proper entrance into society.

As we reach the centre of the foyer, Margie brings our crinoline-galleon to a halt and we create an island of lurid satin in a dark-suited sea. Some of the men around us cluck and chirrup. There is a cry of *my word!* and another, louder, of *oh, yes please!* But Margie has seen the way and she glides us, deftly avoiding a couple of outstretched hands, up on to the staircase.

The lilt of a waltz from inside the auditorium pulls us up. I hum along as I try to rein in the silly smile on my face. The gowns that Margie has had made for us are enormous in their magnificence; satin trails the steps behind us like the secretions of a gorgeously pigmented gastropod. The skirts have perfect proportions for this season, although when I first tried on the new petticoat cage under my gown, Margie had burst out laughing.

'You look like a chaise longue,' she'd tittered.

Now though, resplendent in our full finery, I am counting the gasps of our admirers as we ascend the stairs. We do not fluff our steps or falter. Hours of practice in the new elongated cages has paid off. At the top of the curving stairway I cannot resist a backward glance. All of the eyes upon us, even the ones that seem outraged or averted are most decidedly greedy to see more. Then, my heel catches the edge of the stair. For an instant, I imagine falling backwards and clutching hold of Margie so that our twin-galleon topples and we both tumble down in an indecent waterfall of crinolines and under-things. I snigger at the thought. Lordy, what a sight that would be! Their eyes would be out on stalks!

But Margie, bless her, has an iron grip and steadies me. 'All right, dear?'

'Certainly.'

'Not tipsy, then?'

'As if!'

We both giggle for we have had hardly anything to drink. The only remaining bottle of absinthe in our rooms this afternoon was already about empty.

The crowd parts as we navigate the landing. Fleshy bosoms, some rather sweaty, heave out of our way; a gentleman waves his flattened opera hat to clear us a path. Beside a marble pillar, a bow-legged attendant is clanging the hand-bell. Margie knows exactly where we are going but nevertheless comes to a halt beside him and waits until the ringing has stopped.

'Pray, my man, could you direct us? We have a private box reserved in the name of Mrs Margery Grey.'

The attendant, with a rotten-egg expression, waves an arm toward the corridor behind the dress circle. As we set off, a few youngish men hover behind us like bees around lavender. They are laughing, their hands darting at us, as if wanting to suck some pollen. Margie bats them away quite roughly without breaking her stride.

In a rush of cigar fumes, the door to our box opens. Inside, Figgy and Pollock stand, blustering and a little sheepish. Figgy wipes his mouth as if he has just been stuffing something into it.

'Ladies!'

Pollock moves the chairs and helps us to arrange our cages as we sit.

Margie gives them both a wonderfully supercilious look. 'Gentlemen.'

We invited these beaux, such as they are, to squire us at the theatre on condition that they did not take any of our limelight, and both now look terrified that they may be ejected. Unfurling my fan, I cover my face but they probably can still tell that I am giggling.

The roar of the auditorium is building, as is the odour of bodies. The stalls fill with city-types and swells, matrons and dolled-up shop-girls. Quality squeezes into the dress circle; men in black and white, ladies in chromatic silks, but none of them have gowns so resplendent nor hair-pieces so high as my sister and I.

Above us, three tiers, carved in magenta and gold, ascend to the bellowing gods. My fan flutters as my eyes roam. Gas jets at full glow illuminate the faces turned in our direction. They wear a host of expressions; lascivious or amused, perplexed or hostile. None are indifferent. I marvel, in return, that so few countenances, male or female, might truly be called beautiful. Even fewer, perhaps, shield a radiant soul within. So many in the past have disappointed. But perhaps one such is here, one who is destined for me. I must not give up hope.

My attention is called to the hard seats at the front of the stalls occupied by young men in cheap suits and excessive hair oil.

'Bella, Bella!'

The call comes in a cod-Italian accent from the very front beside the orchestra pit. Two or three saucy types are standing up and gesticulating in our direction. My fan, with an apparent life of its own, begins to vibrate a little faster.

I lean in to Margie. 'Listen, sister. Do you hear? They know my name.'

'What puff and piffle! Don't flatter yourself, dearie.'

'They might.'

'From one of last year's theatre bills still posted to a lamppost?'

'I was mentioned in all the Gaiety's notices.'

Margie rolls her eyes. 'Don't we know it!'

I snap my fan shut and edge myself to the front of the box. As I lean both elbows on the parapet, a cheer comes up from the boys on the hard seats. My eyelids cannot help but flutter and my lace-gloved fingertips give a little wave as they rise to pat to the coils of someone else's hair that balance on my head.

'Give us a smile, Bella!' One of the lads shouts.

'And a song!' Cries another.

I find myself leaning forward over the edge and waving. I even shout something that is not entirely polite. I can't help it.

'Bella!' Margie's voice is stern. 'Have some decorum.'

She is right, of course. And my extravagant waving seems to have sent the boys into a frenzy. They are almost climbing over each other to get nearer to our box. All except for one of them, a tall, shapely young man with deliciously sad eyes. The ushers walk to the front of the pit and point accusing fingers at the rowdy lads before throwing a glance at me. I giggle and cover my face with my fan, but not before blowing a kiss from my lacy fingertips to the sad-eyed youth.

Then, the orchestra strikes up a stirring overture that has the restless crowd settling back into their seats. The gas jets lower a little, but there is still plenty of light reflecting the sheen of my bodice. I sit a little straighter to show my bosom shape to best advantage. We are here to be seen, after all.

The curtain rises and a communal *oh!* escapes from the audience. Even the most enthusiastic gossips are silenced by the marvel that fills the stage. We are all transported, instantly, to ancient Greece. The white columns of a Doric temple adorn the wings and before them, in the agora, youths and nymphs cavort to the eerie strains of a flute, their glorious limbs swathed only in chiffon. In the distance, tiny goats appear to roam across rocky hills and a yellow sun suspended on hardly visible strings pulses real beams onto the turquoise sea. Little boats float so convincingly that it must be actual water.

Into the corner of this scene comes a man, bearded and muscly, carrying a mallet and chisel. As he surveys a huge chunk of rough-hewn marble, he sings of his love for the stone and wonders what his chisel will liberate from its cold heart.

Even in the high tiers, the crowd quietens as the orchestra's melody rises and falls to his plaintive song. We are all mesmerised by the commanding presence of the sculptor and intrigued by the figure that is emerging from the block of marble. Lumps of rock fall away under the sculptor's chisel and slowly, slowly a human form is revealed. It is a female form; slender, naked and as white as the stone from which she is born.

As the final chunk of marble falls to the floor, the sculptor begins to weep. He sings, achingly of his doomed love for this stone maiden, Galatea. She is perfect. And if only she were flesh he would find true earthly fulfilment with her. Briefly, outside the temple, the sculptor's dumpy wife appears with a bad tempered call for him to come home for his dinner. We sense now the coldness and the boredom of the sculptor's marital bed. If only, even for one night, he could share it with a living, pulsing Galatea! With this, he gives the half-formed statue a passionate kiss.

I confess that the sight of this embrace passes a little thrill through my insides. I shift in my seat, glad to be ensconced in my voluminous petticoat cage. As I pat down my skirts, I glance at the cheap seats by the orchestra pit. All of those rosy-faced boys are rapt in the on-stage caress. All except one. The sad-eyed youth is looking up, unblinking, at me. Then he sends from his palm to me, an air-blown kiss. My lips part with longing to receive it.

But on stage, something miraculous has happened. The sculptor's kiss has transformed Galatea into a living being. Although still apparently naked, she is entirely white in the manner of a Grecian statue. The sculptor runs his hands along his creation's curves, lingering on her thighs and breasts. 'Oohs' and chirruping 'aah's' reverberate around the theatre.

A duet starts up now between sculptor and statue accompanied only by the haunting pipes of Pan. *How perfect you are*, he croons, *how well your female form would fit my every need.* She reaches out a hand to stroke his beard. *I can satisfy any man*, she sings, *but only for a brief, fantastical moment. For I am but an illusion. When reality returns, I will again become stone*.

Without warning, Galatea's plaintive words raise a sob from my throat. How beautiful she is, and how tragic her predicament! A hand reaches onto my lap and a soft hankie is pushed into my grasp. Darling Margie is moved too. Her eyes shine in the lowered lights. But we neither of us can bear to meet the other's gaze or we would both collapse weeping into each others arms.

The dancing nymphs circle the temple as sculptor and statue join for one last clinching embrace. But then, with a shrieking aria, the sculptor's fat little wife appears and the interval curtain falls.

As I try to compose myself, my eyes range over the cheap seats. But in a swift move that takes me by surprise, Margie is hoisting me up and pulling me out of the box.

'Quick dearie,' she cries, elbowing Figgy out of the way. 'The bar!'

The doors to the other boxes are still closed and in the corridor Margie picks up her skirts and sets off in a most unladylike manner at a run. The tightness of my stays gives me a stitch in my side but I do my best to keep up with her and keep my dignity. And we are indeed almost the first to arrive at the crush bar.

'What will it be, dear?' Margie is panting but her eyes sparkle. 'A little green fairy?'

'Let's have big green fairies tonight, sister, shall we?'

I start giggling and have trouble bringing it to a stop. Gulping in the piped and perfumed theatre air has made me light-headed.

'Barman, barman! Double absinthe, twice, on the double!' Margie's voice is louder and gruffer than is seemly and I glance around us a trifle warily. One little man in a buttoned-up lounge suit is glaring. As our eyes meet, his moustache twitches. But I refuse to cower. Plenty of others here appreciate our eye-catching attire. Indeed, at this very moment the naughty cadre from the hard seats are coming our way.

'Good evening, ladies.' The loudest of them, a very pink-faced youth, comes so close that his leg pushes into my skirts. 'May we buy you a drink.'

Margie, handing me a bulbous glass of green slosh, has already heard. 'Barman, this gentleman here will settle the bill for us.'

Pinky-face grins and pushes his leg deeper into my scarlet folds. His hand goes up towards mine but I do not loosen my hold on the fan. He settles for stroking his knuckle against the strip of bare white forearm above my glove. I do not object. We will call it payment for the absinthe.

'What is your name, sweetheart?' He says with a chirrup. Clearly, he thinks I am a whore.

'Bella Marchant,' I reply. 'Do you not recognise me?'

'Should I?'

For a moment he looks panicked, as if we have had some past drunken triste which has escaped his recollection.

'I am quite well known on the London stage.'

'Oh.' A look of relief passes over his face and he licks his lips as he tries to decide how next to press his suit. So many men think that an actress and a whore are the same thing. But absinthe or not, he will not be buying any more of me tonight.

'Ah, here are our beaux. Figgy! Pollock!' I raise my closed fan in the air and wave it in their direction. Then I step away from pinky-face.

At moments like this Figgy and Pollock have their uses. It is sometimes shocking how badly two ladies about town have need of gentlemen escorts. But then, as Figgy squeezes in beside me, I see a pair of long-lashes flickering above his shoulder. It is the sad-eyed youth. Elbowing Figgy aside, I beckon him forward and with a flick my skirts I open a crevice between me and the bar into which the lovely youth may slip.

'That's right, dear boy, come closer and let us be introduced.'

'Oh, I know who you are, Miss.' His long-lashed boldness is entrancing.

'You do?'

'I saw you in Peep O'Day. Miss. You were a marvel.'

'Ah.' I am already beaming. I cannot help it. Although I have never acted in that particular production. For a moment I am distracted by trying to recall which actress he must have mistaken me for. 'Thank you Mr…'

'Judd. Mr Jeremy Judd.'

'I am charmed, Mr Jeremy Judd.'

I put out my hand and he takes it, holding onto my fingers as he continues to look into my eyes.

'You may kiss it, Jeremy, if you like.' There is a second of confusion before he lifts my hand to his mouth. Through the lace, I feel the urgent hotness of his lips. I lean forward and put my own mouth to his ear. 'You are a pet. And you may come and visit me after the show.'

'I…I…'

He seems shocked. Perhaps I have gone too far. The lady he has mistaken me for must have been more coy. I continue as if I have said nothing untoward.

'Are you are a regular theatre-goer Mr Judd?'

'I should say so.'

'And your taste is for extravaganzas?'

'Why yes, and ordinary operas too.'

'And how do you rate tonight's show?'

'Oh...capital! The scene between the sculptor and the statue was...was...'

'Delicious?'

He nods, apparently unable to speak.

'Love such as theirs is the most exquisite sort…a love that must be enjoyed fleetingly and in secret before the lady once again takes on her natural state.'

A tremor of confusion passes across Jeremy's eyes.

But at that moment I sense, amidst the press of bodies at the bar, a scuffle that is throwing up a plume of emerald silk. Margie's voice, throaty and fearful rises above the melee.

'Take your horrible hand…'

My eyes see what is happening but my mind refuses to believe it. The little buttoned up man with the moustache has grabbed Margie's wrist. Smoke from her lighted cigarette draws figures of eight in the air as she tries to wrestle her hand free. The little man's cheeks are becoming very red. Margie's arm is evidently stronger than his. But then his more burly friend in a bowler hat arrives and yanks both of her arms behind her back.

Margie's more feminine attempts at protest desert her. 'Take your bleeding hands off me you bastards!'

But the men hold fast, and in a flash of understanding that makes me start to back away I see exactly what is happening. Too late! A third policemen comes alongside me.

'Now then, you're going to come nicely aren't you, and not make a pointless fuss like your friend?'

A pong of male armpits seeps from his jacket.

'But we have done nothing wrong.'

'Oh yes you have.'

'What?'

'You present an affront to public morals. So you must accompany us Bow Street Police Station.'

'Now?'

He chuckles and puts his hairy hand on my naked elbow. I know better than to shake it off. I let him steer me through the crush around the bar and down the staircase. My eyes stay lowered. I most certainly do not wish to meet any of those leering stares. And I cannot bear that any of them may be Jeremy's. As we shiver on to the pavement, a cold drench of shame numbs me against the laughs and taunts that greet us. Margie is still tustling with the plain-clothes men, which only prolongs our ordeal. One of them hails a cab and I see Margie's face streaked with powdery black tears as she is bundled into it.

Another cab comes up behind and the horse prances as it is reined hard toward the kerb. With a little *oh!* I lurch back against the sweaty policeman. His nails dig into my flesh and twist. For a terrifying moment I think I might cry. But then I am thrust up into the hansom, petticoat cage flying. There is a sickening rip of satin. The sound pulls a solitary tear from the corner of my eye.

The cab is dark though, and mercifully, Constable Stinky-pits does not speak to me on the short journey to Bow Street. He sits with arms folded, a disgusted sneer plastered to his face. I bite back the urge to tell him that, actually, the nasty odour in the cab originates in his own bodily recesses.

The cab swings to a halt. Scruffy lads crowd around the columns at the entrance to the police station. Perhaps they have been drawn like moths to Margie's flame. Or perhaps there is always an audience for whatever human flotsam the constables bring in on a Saturday night. It is entertainment, I suppose, and cheaper than the gods.

As I step down from the cab, I see, with a shudder, that I will have to push my way through the jostle of bodies. Then, one of the lads catches sight of me and shouts out.

'Mary-Ann! Mary-Ann! Sing us a song!

Somehow, I do not know quite how, I flash the blighter a dazzling smile. And like magic, the crush parts to let me through. The lads seem suddenly unsure of why I am here, and of what I am.

Inside, the police station is grander than the one at King Street. Gas-lit orbs glare onto the high desk that runs along the back of the reception hall. Drunks and ne'er do wells crowd the benches and policemen in high-collared jackets engage them in loud banter. The quips, on both sides, sound theatrical as if rehearsed.

I am pushed into one of the wooden docks that front the desk. The waist-high door is bolted behind me as if I am a heffer at Smithfield market. A bald sergeant looms.

'Name.'

I wince. It is the question I have been dreading. The sergeant leans forward and a spot of white light moves over his pate. His piggy features grow menacing.

'Once more. But only once, mind you. Name!'

I swallow. 'Would a stage name be acceptable?'

Perhaps there is some statute which might allow 'Bella Marchant' to be my valid appellation.

'No, it would not.'

His eyes narrow and I know this could be my last chance to speak before being hauled away. I am suddenly and ineffably weary of pretence.

'Alfred Billings.'

The sergeant snorts. 'Quite so.' His features loosen into a self-satisfied smile. 'Abode?'

'Haxell's Hotel, West Strand.'

'Is that your fixed abode?'

I nod. But I must appear equivocal.

'I said, is that your fixed abode?'

'No. I usually live with my father, Charles Billings, a bank manager, at 15 Bruton Crescent.'

'Ooh, la-di- da!'

The sergeant's attempt at a high-pitched he-she voice makes my insides run cold. What amusements I wonder, do they have in store for us? My heart quakes for poor Margie. She will not be able to contain her rage at their provocations and will work herself into a fearful state.

The sergeant looks at his paperwork then nods at a boy in a policeman's uniform. 'Yard cells. Number four.'

As the boyish constable jerks back the dock bolt, I am jolted into speech. 'But what charge is there? What have we done wrong?'

The officers exchange a look and then both explode with laughter. The sergeant's laugh turns into a belch as he glances at his paperwork.

'It says here, *outrage to public decency*. That will do for now. No doubt there'll be more to add once we've had a proper look at you.'

He gives the constable a wink that seems filled with pure evil.

The boy-constable leads me, with a rather limp hand on my elbow, through a corridor reeking of carbolic and puke then down stone steps into a dank yard. The cells that line the yard might once have been stables. A flutter of hope passes through me as the door of number four clanks open. Will Margie be inside? At least then we could cling together and weep into each other's sisterly bosom. But instead, waiting for me inside the stark cell, are two policemen and a grey-bearded man in a black frock coat who is holding a leather bag.

The key clunks in the lock and the constable lets go of my arm. The cell is large. Perhaps it was once a loose box. The furniture is sparse though, with a low pallet covered by a grey blanket at one side, and in the middle of the room, a scrubbed table upon which an oil lamp burns. There is a grille in the door but no windows. An iron bucket seems to serve as the privy.

'Right then. Let's see what we have here.' The constable's babyish countenance seems suddenly sinister. He turns to me and for a second his eyes lock on to mine. 'Strip.'

Inside the petticoat cage, my legs buckle. I want to ask what he means but the instruction is unutterably clear.

I falter and lean a hand on the table. 'I cannot.'

The baby-face contorts into gargoyle of outrage. 'What?'

I try a slightly deeper voice with a soupcon of bonhomie. 'What I mean to say, sir, gentlemen, is that the bodice of my gown fastens at the back. With tiny hooks. I cannot reach them.'

The constable shakes his head. 'Are you saying that you require one of these fine officers of the Metropolitan constabulary to act as your ladies' maid?'

The other two policemen exchange smirks and the man in the frock coat raises an eyebrow. I lower my head and nod.

At this, the constable leers and points at the taller of his two colleagues. 'Price, you're married so you should know what to do. Assist the prisoner.'

Constable Price steps forward and takes off his helmet, placing it on the table. Behind his sandy moustache, his face reddens but his eyes are hard. He jerks me round so that my back is to the light and begins to work on my fastenings. To make his job easier, I breathe in. I find that I can hold my breath for much longer than I thought possible. It helps me to concentrate on something other than the eyes that are all trained greedily on to my bosom. I wish as I exhale, that I might never take another breath again, but air, unbidden, inflates my ribcage. And soon, every hook has vacated its eye and my bodice falls loosely away. The constable takes it from me and throws it on top of my creamy stole that lies rumpled on the damp floor.

The boy constable was right. Price is expert in the removal of ladies' clothing. Deftly he loosens the strings and buttons inside my skirt so that it opens and wilts to the ground like overblown rose petals. Price bends to my feet as I step out of the skirt and I find myself putting a hand on his shoulder. He does not seem to object. Silken folds are bundled up and thrown onto the pile where they lie slick as blood in the lamplight.

Stripped of finery, only my white under-things remain. Price works on; unhooking, unlacing, unbuttoning. Flannel then calico, my petticoats fall away and the cage drops, deflated into flatness. The policemen's smirks and quips harden into more avid attention. Lips are licked. And as the laces of my corset loosen, the cell's silence is pregnant with expectation.

I have a piercing memory of Galatea. How similar to that marble goddess I now am! With each chip of falling stone her lovely nakedness was revealed to the audience's impatient eyes. Price, as he peels away the stiffness of my stays and lets the bosomy wadding fall to the floor, is my sculptor. The final cotton petticoat drops; the stockings unfurl. Only the short cotton shift remains to cover my naturalness. Price steps away.

The boy-constable coughs, then flicks his hand in my direction. 'Go on then. Take it off.'

They expect me, no doubt, to object. Or at least to say something jokey. But I will not give them that satisfaction. I stand up straight. I am Galatea; I am beautiful, I am beloved. And so I feel no shame. Nor do I even feel the cold as I raise my shift over my head and stand naked before the policemen.

And the gasp they disgorge could be that of the theatre-goers as they glimpse the nude Galatea.

'Blow me!'

The baby-faced constable is unable to contain himself. But as Galatea, I do not feel even slightly tempted to make the obvious riposte.

He coughs again. 'Beg pardon, Doctor. Shall we proceed to the examination?'

The man in the frock coat nods. I have a sudden horrible presentiment of what is coming. But I will be Galatea. I will stay in her form; innocent, otherworldly, serene, and she will protect me.

Price and his pal then each grab of one of my arms. The boy-constable lifts away the oil lamp as they push me face down onto the deal table, ramming my privates against the splintery edge. I see the frock coat pass by as the doctor moves behind me. The boy-constable accompanies him, carrying the lamp. Presently, unseen hands prise my buttocks painfully apart and I feel the burning warmth of the oil-lamp just above my skin.

But I do not flinch. I do not utter the slightest cry. I do not even listen to the doctor's muttered words; *dilated* and *sodomised* and *unnatural*. Because I am still Galatea, a statue of ethereal gorgeousness, and all who look upon my nakedness cannot fail to fall in love.

This statue-magic will work, I have no doubt, upon the most surprising of subjects. Perhaps even upon an upright young man who thinks himself in thrall to a pretty actress. And tomorrow, as I cross Bow Street from police station to court, I may see amidst the jeering rabble a pair of long-lashed sad eyes. My hairdo will be dishevelled and my torn gown at the back. Stubble may even shadow my cheek. But he will not mind. And even though he will no longer have any doubt about what I am, Jeremy Judd will raise his soft palm in my direction and blow Galatea a kiss.

Carolyn Kirby is a novelist and the author of *The Conviction of Cora Burns.*

France in the Second World War: An Enduring Myth, by Alex Gerlis

In his latest spy novel, *Agent in the Shadows*, the third Wolf Pack, Alex Gerlis has taken us to occupied France. Here he describes the challenges of writing about a particularly brutal war that is often misunderstood.

I've written extensively on the Second World War in Europe. My eleven books may be works of fiction but the plots are all based around real events that unfolded during the war. That history and the locations I use are all carefully researched. I scrupulously avoid altering the history or any other facts to fit the plots: it's an important principle that they have to work around the real events and places and not the other way round.

My novels cover most of the countries in Europe during 1939-1945: the United Kingdom and Germany; the countries which fell under Nazi occupation and the Soviet Union which of course spent the war in different camps and just as importantly, the five neutral countries (including Turkey).

What I always try to bring across in my books is the complexity of the war, both in terms of how countries behaved during it and how their populations responded to events – the human side of the conflict. Within the obvious parameters of the war unquestionably being between the Allies and the Axis countries – between good and evil - I try hard to avoid a simplistic black and white approach, when in reality so much of what occurred in Europe in this period was so much more complex than this.

And this brings me to my main point. In my opinion, the most complex country during the Second World War was France. One of the main themes of my latest novel – *Agent in the Shadows* – is what I describe as 'the fraught topic of collaboration with the Nazis in France during the war'. Linked to this is the equally difficult subject of the effectiveness of the French resistance during the war, famously described by General Dwight Eisenhower, as having been worth 'an extra six divisions'.

And history has in many ways been kind to France since 1945, arguably overplaying the impact of the resistance before 1944 and playing down the extent of collaboration with the Nazis throughout the war.

For a good deal of the war the French resistance operated very much on the margins as well as in the shadows. 'For a long period of the war' as I say in my book 'the Resistance was little more than an annoyance for the German occupiers and limited in its effectiveness.'

Indeed, the Nazi occupation of France began on 10th May 1940 but it would be another 15 months before the first German was killed by the Resistance, when a young *résistant* called Pierre Georges (better known by his subsequent *nom de guerre*, Colonel Fabien) shot dead a German naval officer at Barbès-Rochechouart metro station in the Montmartre district of Paris on 21st August 1941.

When Paris was liberated on 25th August 1944 the business of myth-making began on the same the day. General de Gaulle addressed large crowds from the Hôtel de Ville, telling them France had been 'liberated by her own people, with the help of the armies of France, with the help and support of the whole of France, that is to say of fighting France, that is to say of the true France, the eternal message'.

It was a message which somehow managed to ignore the role played by the British, US and Canadian armies along with Polish and other troops in liberating France. It also failed to mention the Resistance: at that time de Gaulle was desperately worried by what he saw as a communist-dominated organisation which was a threat to his authority.

It also failed to acknowledge what is an interest footnote in the liberation of Paris, one that took many years to be acknowledged and is still little known about. The city was liberated on 25 August by US Army Fifth Corps and the Second Armored Division of the Free French Army. However, the night before the 9th Company of the Free French defied orders and entered the city by the Porte d'Italie, thus becoming the first Allied troops to enter the city.

The 9th Company was commanded by Captain Raymond Dronne, but around 150 of the 160 in his men were in fact Spanish Republicans, so much so that they were known as La Nueve. It is believed that a Spanish officer – Amado Grannell, a veteran of the Spanish Civil War – was the first officer to enter the city.

It's perhaps not surprising that de Gaulle failed to mention this. As far as he was concerned, Paris – and the whole of France – had been liberated by the French people, rising as one, as they had been throughout the war. It had not been liberated by the resistance, or the Allied armies and certainly not by Spanish Republicans.

This then, was the myth. The myth has also come to include not just the extent of collaboration during the war but also the way it was dealt with after it.

Much of the collaboration could be described as low level, or indirect, but nonetheless vital for a successful occupation of France by the Nazis. For a good deal of the war much of the French population was content to live their lives as before, not wanting to cause too much trouble. In some areas, the resistance was regarded as trouble makers. Then there was the more direct collaboration, better termed as treason.

After the war this was dealt with by the *épuration*, which translates as 'the purification'. There were two main phases to the *épuration*. The first phase was the unofficial one, known as the *épuration sauvage,* where the resistance and other groups administered summary justice to those they saw as collaborators. There is no exact figure as to how many were executed in this phase, which is perhaps an indication of how this period has now been forgotten. Estimates of those killed in this phase vary enormously, from a conservative estimate of around 10,000 to others which put the number executed as being over 100,000.

The *épuration* légale, the official treatment of collaborators. According to Ian Ousby in Occupation, in the period 1944-1953 160,287 people were tried for collaboration. Only a quarter of them were actually convicted and imprisoned. A further 7,037 were sentenced to death, with that sentence actually carried out for just 1,500 of them.

Three weeks after the liberation of Paris de Gaulle arrived in newly-liberated Lyon and addressed the crowds on Place des Terreaux on 14th September. But this time he could hardly ignore the Resistance, describing the city as '*...la capitale de la Résistance Française...*' He went on to say: 'How to tell Lyon all the emotion, all the gratitude I feel in this Gallic capital, which was the capital of the French Resistance and which is today a very large city in our France covered with wounds, shining in its honour and carried away by its hope.'

But there was no mention of a profound betrayal which had taken place just a couple of miles north of where de Gaulle was standing that day. And it's all the more surprising given his own personal interest in the case. By 1942, the somewhat disorganised and ineffective nature of the resistance along with its internal rivalries had been a matter of deep concern to de Gaulle. He was convinced that properly organised it could play a major role in undermining the German occupation – and be an important force when the Allies landed in France, both of which proved to be true.

In March 1943 de Gaulle sent his emissary Jean Moulin to France with a brief to unify the resistance. It was natural that Moulin should seek to do this in Lyon, which certainly while that part of France came under Vichy had been the capital of the Resistance.

Moulin began to make progress: on 21 June 1943 – operating under the code name 'Max' – he organised a meeting of the National Council of the Resistance at a doctor's surgery in Caluire-et-Cuire in the north of Lyon. The meeting was about to begin when the surgery was raided by the Gestapo, led by the notorious Klaus Barbie, the 'Butcher of Lyon'.

One of the nine Resistance leaders there somehow managed to escape, though he was later recaptured. The rest were taken to the Gestapo prison in Lyon, Fort Montluc. Barbie soon discovered that 'Max' was the man who'd been hunted throughout France. Jean Moulin was subjected to dreadful torture and died as a result of this a fortnight later.

But who had betrayed the meeting? My fictionalised take on this is at the heart of the plot of *Agent in the Shadows*. There is a general, if reluctant agreement that it was most probably betrayed by one of the attendees: the French resistance had a strict protocol regarding meetings, realising they were the times when they were most exposed: generally, only those invited to a meeting would be aware of it and even then, they would be given the details as late as possible. But if there's an agreement as to who was the traitor, there's no consensus as to who it was.

Many people suspected René Hardy, who escaped during the raid although was later captured. He survived the war, after which he was twice put on trial for his complicity in the raid and twice acquitted. Suspicion has also fallen on Raymond Aubrac who was arrested at the surgery and imprisoned but who later escaped from the Gestapo. Aubrac was a leading communist and there was a feeling that the communists resented de Gaulle gaining control of the Resistance – which up to then they'd been the most powerful element.

In many ways it is astonishing that eighty years on, the identity of the traitor is as much a mystery now as it was then. More than once, when researching my novel, I was warned that this was a subject I ought not address. Perhaps this is one of those rare examples of where fiction is an acceptable way of addressing an unresolved controversy.

Alex Gerlis is the bestselling author of *The Wolf Pack Spies*, the latest of which is *Agent in the Shadows*.

Renegade's Tale: John Sayles Interview.

Two-time Oscar nominee John Sayles is well-known for writing and directing his own features most of which have a strong historical theme. He has recently written an epic novel, *Jamie MacGillivray*, which begins during the Jacobite Rebellion of 1745 and our editor met him recently to discuss the book, its history and Hollywood today.

I first watched *Lone Star* soon after it came out in 1996. This atmospheric film, centred on a small-town grappling with its past, is both a whodunnit and a social commentary. The town in question was in Texas and where three communities, White European, African American and Mexican American were still learning to live together after a traumatic past. It was clear its writer and director had a strong appreciation of history, and so when I learnt John Sayles had written a new novel, set in 18th century Scotland, England, Martinique, Canada and America I was keen to meet him. The Highlands and the '45 did not seem to be a natural area of interest for an American filmmaker, but the mention of one name, an actor, soon cleared that up.

'Robert Carlyle, the Scottish actor, called me up…about a Highlander who was defeated at the Battle of Culloden. Instead of hanging him, they transported him to the New World and he got involved with the Sioux Indians. I said, "Well, if he lives to be 200, he'll get involved with the Sioux Indians. But there's plenty of Indians that were encountered on the East Coast. And I just liked the idea so much I…wrote a screenplay for Robert to be in, and we came over to Scotland and toured the Highlands and we scouted in Georgia and Florida for those locations. We scouted in Canada, and just were never - it was…an epic movie…but we never were able to raise the money for it. And so some 20 years later, I just felt like… I still love that story. And I went back into it.'

And what a story it is, taking the reader from the battlefield in the Highlands to the New World via London, the West Indies and Nova Scotia. He's quite right, it is an epic. There is something hugely seductive about the frontiers of those American colonies prior to the American Revolution and the establishment of a new country. The story deals with native tribes, Highlanders and Native Americans, bumping up against a technologically more advanced adversary.

'…What I was trying to get at in the book is that…in the States…our history was most: civilised people came over to this country and encountered savages…Mostly in the movies that I saw when I was a kid, it seemed like all they did was dance around the fire at night, and then go scalp white people. Their cultures were not represented in any way. And one of the things that I learned over the years as I got interested in it, is that the native cultures, especially on the East Coast, at that time, were highly evolved. There was what we call the Iroquois Confederacy, which was five and eventually six or seven tribes that came together to rule their area - very complicated diplomatic politics with other tribes around them. Very complicated. The economy, because all of a sudden, there were these goods that they could have. Rifles instead of bows and arrows and steel pots instead of having to make six pots out of clay every year and they got hooked on those consumer goods. All of a sudden, they had to kill a lot more deer than they used to, just to eat and wear. And all of a sudden, they're in their enemy's territory, poaching their deer and their enemies are in their territory, poaching their deer; and then there's a whole beaver-thing where beaver hats get popular in Europe. The beavers disappear, and they're killing each other over beavers. So, it was just as complicated as the War of Austrian Succession, which you hear about in the book.'

We do, and in it Sayles, through the hero Jamie MacGillivray, gives a quite beautifully pithy summary of the causes and state of play of that war between the Old World nations. But since the book began as a screenplay, and is now an epic novel, clearly new elements of the story emerge?

'What happens when you do that with a screenplay, of course, is it starts to expand. And so the character of Jenny, who in the screenplay was on seven pages, appeared and reappeared once more - she becomes a third of the book when I discovered there were some women transported and one of the boats was taken by a French Privateer…freed in Martinique, and I thought of this starving barefoot girl, all of a sudden in Martinique, and there's mangoes and good food and it is a totally different culture and a new language and she's one of those people who is absolutely uneducated, but adventurous and really smart.'

Jenny, a Highlander too, meets and comes under the protection of a French Army officer in the French colony, so adding the West Indies to the tale. With the two main characters having suffered so terribly under their Hanoverian overlords, they are quick to ally themselves to Britain's natural enemy. There is a savagery of this period that is captured so effectively by Sayles – something that Ian Mortimer (see cover feature) would presumably be happy with.

'I learned about bloody law in in the Britain of that time, in the Three Kingdoms, I realised, "who are the savages here?" They're still hanging people until they're not quite dead, and then eviscerating and throwing their entrails on a fire - so the dying person can see their entrails! And all before they cut their head off and put it on a spike. So, one of the one of the things that was going is this idea of what exactly is savagery? What exactly?'

The similarity between the Scottish clans and the Native American tribes is an interesting one.

'The clan system has a lot of parallels with some of the more or less evolved, politically, tribes in [America] at the time…I always had this idea that one of the modes of survival, if you are a linguist, if you are good at languages, you are valuable, and you might be able to survive by your wits… "I can speak French and English, and now I can speak, Lenape." And those treaties between the natives in America, and Europeans very often, there were six languages or so being spoken, because nobody spoke one to one, and of course, things get distorted - about land and life and war and tribute…The Indians wanted to understand what we're making our mark on. But they might have to go through Mohawk to Lenape to German to Dutch to English to French."

The language aspect of the novel makes it even more rich, with Erse (Scots Gaelic) as well as other Native American languages being spoken. There is even a character who becomes valued by a particular tribe because he has learnt their language and can then pass down their stories of the past, playing the role of their Homer.

Of course, since Sayles is a distinguished filmmaker, I was keen to get his view of Hollywood today. The seemingly endless superhero films are a source of some frustration to me. Are the studios running out of ideas?

'Well, for one thing is studios are on their last legs. Most of them have been bought by corporations - Warner Brothers is now a big part of a conglomerate. The idea is market research and the money people are definitely at the wheel. What they have decided is, it's really hard to get people into a theatre, and the one thing that they can make that gets people into the theatre are continuing stories. So it might be *Thor: Ragnarok*, it might be *Spiderman*, it might be *Indiana Jones*, it might be the dinosaurs from *Jurassic Park*. But if we make one of those, we have a guaranteed audience. A certain number of people are going to come.

'The best work is being done on TV series. Much better in Europe than in the States, but still…there are some very good series happening here and they're coming from the streamers. I've seen five movies since COVID ended in theatres and they've been screenings. There are 300 seats and five of us there.

'It's another *Mission Impossible* with Tom Cruise or a sequel to *Top Gun*. It's a proven commodity, whereas something new, a new drama, who knows? It could be the best drama in the world. And we can't get people in. So the economics have always driven in it.'

As I mentioned at the start, *Lone Star* is one of his films that I love, but with the above in mind, I wondered if it would be made today? What Sayles has to say saddens me, as it seems such a waste of talent.

'It's really hard for me. I'm just not on the list right now. That's just age and some of that's track record that I have never made, in the last 20 years, anybody any money. Things might have done well, but not if you make $2 million for people they're not interested in Hollywood. They're there to make $20 to $100 million in profit. We could put it in the bank and the interest would be $2 million. So what if we wasted our time on with me as a director? Somebody else might be able to direct who had just had a hit and could take that very screenplay and get it made. They probably would have to cast it differently. Chris Cooper probably wouldn't be the lead. Somebody who had had a big hit recently would be the lead. We were very lucky. Sometimes we got independent funding. Twice I worked with the studio and once it was terrible and once it was fine. But that was a different time.'

Sayles now has *Jamie MacGillivray* which would make a wonderful TV series, even if Robert Carlyle is a bit too long in the teeth to play the lead, but perhaps the 'Auld Fox', Lord Lovat who makes an appearance in the novel?

'They just have to spend the money. And from the *Outlander* series, the costumes are in a wardrobe somewhere. They could use some of those…[Carlyle] would be in it, but I'd like to get him involved somewhere. It's so much fun to imagine travelling around the Highlands of Scotland with Robert Carlyle to knock on doors with you.'

A happy thought, and so who knows, perhaps we'll see *Jamie MacGillivray* in a Netflix series out soon.

John Sayles is a writer, producer and director of a many critically acclaimed films including *Lone Star* (1996), *Eight Men Out* (1988), *Passion Fish* (1992) and *Go for Sisters* (2013). He is the author of six novels, the latest being *Jamie MacGillivray: The Renegade's Journey*. You can listen to an extended version of the interview on the Aspects of History Podcast.

Book Reviews

Medieval Horizons: Why the Middle Ages Matter, by Ian Mortimer

Review by Paul Bernardi

Accessible, fascinating, and illuminating are just three of the adjectives that spring to mind when discussing *Medieval Horizons*. To sum up the basic premise of the book, if I can do it justice in a few words… Mortimer seeks to challenge the lazy and established view that not much happened in the Middle Ages. That if Rip van Winkle had fallen asleep in the year 1000, he would not have had much trouble fitting in had he awoken in the year 1600. There is a view that all of the accoutrements of modern life and modern thinking are the result of the great strides made in the last two hundred and fifty years or so.

What follows is then an enjoyable romp through many facets of life in the Medieval period, ranging from war, religion, equality (or, rather, inequality), literacy, self-awareness and travel to name a few. In each sphere, Mortimer seeks to encourage the reader to challenge their beliefs, to open their minds to the great advances in thinking, human endeavour and the way of life that took place over the 600 year period in question. Developments which have been, all too often, pushed into the shadows in favour of more appealing stories about combustion engines, space travel, the internet and the like.

To give but one example, Mortimer suggests that an eleventh century peasant appearing in London at the end of Queen Elizabeth I's reign would be more likely to be stunned by the buildings, the books, the plentiful food, the ability to buy things that you needed rather than make them yourself and so on. So agog might they be that they might not even notice the ring-tone on a time-travelling smart phone.

It is inarguable that we have seen immense changes in the last two to three centuries; and the pace of change seems to be ever increasing. But to not ask what laid the foundation for these advances is to do the Middle Ages a disservice. To think of the time from 1000 to 1600 as somehow backward, violent and dominated only by superstition is to ignore the light that shone into the corners. To recall – as Mortimer does – Ving Rhames in *Pulp Fiction* threatening to "get Medieval on your ass" should really be seen – after reading this book – as a positive and enlightening outcome for the gentleman concerned.

Paul Bernardi is an author of novels set during the Norman invasion, the latest of which is *Blood Price*.

Iron and Blood: A Military History of the German-Speaking Peoples since 1500, by Peter H. Wilson

Review by Gordon Corrigan

For military historians the top of the academic greasy pole is the Chichele Chair of The History of War at Oxford, and so one would expect any work emanating from that source to be the definitive work of its subject. *Iron and Blood* by Professor Peter H. Wilson is certainly that. A magisterial study covering the development of the art of war amongst German speakers – by which he means the pre-unification German states, Germany itself, Austria and Switzerland – over five centuries, this is an enormously wide-ranging survey of over 900 pages including notes and the index. It charts the development of the German art, or science, of war from the Holy Roman Empire to the 2022 invasion of Ukraine. The author not only describes the strictly military actions and wars of the period, but crucially he explains how and why each protagonist arrived at the point of military engagement. In this he looks at the development of recruitment, weaponry, tactics, intelligence gathering and administration, as well as the wider issues of politics, theology, morality, motivation, welfare and the conventions that led to accepted practices and ultimately to the laws of armed conflict.

One thread throughout the book is that while accepting that militarism has been an integral factor throughout German history, the author denies that there is some inherent martial quality in the German character. Rather, Wilson points out that pre-unification Prussia did not possess any particular genius for war but others thought it did. German participation in all of the major wars of the period are well described: the Thirty Years War (and here he punctures some of the accepted myths of the Peace of Westphalia); the Nine Years War; the Seven Years War; the French Revolutionary and Napoleonic Wars; the Wars of German Unification; as well as numerous other engagements, some of which will have escaped the attention of many historians. The author is adamant that the German error in both world wars was in allowing a separation of the political and the military dimensions, which led to embarking on war with no end strategy in sight, a search for a victory without knowing what to do with it. Wilson feels that historically German military commanders have been too concerned with the operational and tactical levels without thought to the wider, strategic, implications.

The maps are excellent, as is the selection of plates. One can, of course, arrive at differing conclusions from the same evidence and inevitably, in a work of this magnitude, there will be points of dispute. It might also be argued that Germany lost both world wars not because the Russian, British, French or American soldier or army was more competent than the German, when all the evidence would indicate that he and it were not, but simply because Germany could not possibly prevail by taking on so many enemies all at once. Factors of population, geography, economics and industrial base determined that. But these are minor quibbles in what is a magnificent and very readable explanation of a grand sweep of history, which brings us right up to date and is unlikely ever to be bettered.

Gordon Corrigan is a military historian and author of *The Second World War: A Military History*.

The Lighthouse of Stalingrad, by Iain MacGregor

Review by Trevor James

Towards the end of this very engaging book, Iain MacGregor reveals the central focus of his chosen title. Indeed, he explains both the main title and his by-line - *The Hidden Truth at the Centre of WWII's Greatest Battle'*. In the midst of the grim and devastating battle of Stalingrad, Junior Sergeant Yakov Pavlov was reported to have withstood the German attack at a very prominent building on the front line, and subsequently he was heralded and honoured within the Soviet Union as a hero of that epic struggle. What MacGregor reveals, of course, is that this celebration was very much a product of Soviet propaganda and, in reality, whilst Pavlov did exist and did occupy the structure now known as the 'lighthouse', there is little substance to the narrative of what he is reported to have achieved. We are presented with a classic example of how an attractive and heroic story can be moulded into an image that can inspire national pride. This represents an attempt to explain the enormity of what had happened and how disaster, albeit at a massive cost, had been averted. Lack of detail or indeed substance does not remove the impact of such a propagandist narrative, and once the 'legend' is established in the public mind it is very difficult to dislodge. Enough detail existed to justify the start of the 'legend' and then it becomes self-sustaining. My personal parallel is Winston Churchill's heroic escape from the Boers at Ladysmith in 1899: it did happen but we have always been rather short on detail.

Having so far focussed on the central object of this book, this work also offers the present-day reader a great deal more. Although we sense that we know what happened at Stalingrad, with its desperately high death toll and the Germans proving the truth of that long-standing dictum that supply lines can only be stretched so far, Iain MacGregor offers us a very balanced approach to what happened.

Considering the battle planning and organisation on both sides in an even-handed manner was very helpful for this non-military historian. In describing the strategies of the various military forces involved, this book has given me a much greater understanding of how the stalemate developed and ultimately was resolved, even with the detail of how their relative positions developed along the banks of the River Volga becoming much more clear.

Another highly commendable of quality of Iain MacGregor's research is his use of contemporary testimonies. Diary comments from both sides added strongly to what we can know of how the people felt about what was happening. In particular, the extensive use of material from General Friedrich Roske is extraordinarily valuable. In utilising the letters and memoirs of the man who was at the heart of the German command at the point of surrender and who then was taken into captivity until 1955 is very poignant. Through his eyes we can really appreciate how the German position began to become untenable and how the final surrender became inevitable.

This is a major contribution to our understanding of how the war on the Eastern Front played its part in the eventual demise of the Nazi regime.

Trevor James is a historian and former Secretary of the Historical Association.

Colonialism: A Moral Reckoning, by Nigel Biggar

Review by Robert Lyman

This is an important, timely and brave book. It is the first serious counter blast against the hysterical and ahistorical orthodoxy that has placed such a stranglehold on our public discourse on the British Empire, and as such will prove to be an indispensable handbook in the battles to come. It will no doubt be rejected out of hand by those who hold the view that imperialism and its sister 'ism', colonialism, are morally irredeemable and that therefore the sort of exercise undertaken by Biggar is itself morally suspect.

While other motives played a part, it was social, religious and political motives which drove the colonial endeavour in the New World from the 1620s; security and religious issues which drove the subjugation of Catholic (and therefore Royalist) Ireland in the 1650s; social and administrative factors which led to the settlement in Australia from 1788 and social and religious imperatives which drove the colonisation of New Zealand in the 1840s. In circumstances where trade and the security of trade was the primary motive for imperialism – think of Clive in the 1750s for example – a wide variety of outcomes ensued. In India, Clive's defeat of the Nawab Siraj-ud-daulah in 1757 was in support of a palace coup that placed Siraj's uncle Mir Jafar on the throne of Bengal, thus allowing the East India Company the precious favoured trading status that Siraj had previously rejected. This led in time to the Company gradually taking over the administrative functions of the Bengal state and, to seek to protect its new prerogatives, providing security from both internal and external threats (the Mahratta raiders, for example). So we see the incremental, almost accidental, accrual of power that began in the early 1600s, step into colonial administration a century and a half later and then lead to the transfer of power across a great swathe of the Indian sub-continent to the British Crown in 1858.

I agree with Biggar that a remarkable legacy of the British exercise of empire was to introduce standards of probity in public administration and governance that was unparalleled in the history of imperialism, even if this legacy was tarnished by the horrors, for instance, of Amritsar and the Bengal famine. India, along with most other parts of the empire, received its independence as a 'going concern' from its imperial parent in 1947. One measure of the success of this transfer is the extent to which India retained the civic and governmental structures it inherited. It is remarkable to see how much this is in fact the case. In my area of study, it is fascinating to see how the people of the Naga Hills in Assam were irritated by the arrival of the British in the 1870s (because they inhibited the traditional culture of inter-tribal warfare and headhunting) but angered by their departure in 1947. That rancour – about Britain leaving – exists to this day. The history of colonialism – and imperialism – is complicated.

This book is a beautifully written and thought-provoking analysis of Britain's imperial and colonial history from a moral perspective. Biggar has challenged all of us, historians and others, to recognise that motives, context and agency are as critical to understand the past as they are to evaluate the present. In particular, his book challenges the motives of those who seek to destroy Britain's faith in itself by asserting dogmatically that its past is nothing to be proud of and that we have no right to assert moral virtue as a nation *because* of our past. His book will set the cat among the pigeons, but only if the pigeons are prepared to have their orthodoxy challenged.

Robert Lyman is a historian and author of the acclaimed *A War of Empires: Japan, India, Burma and Britain 1941 – 1945.*

The Path of Peace: Walking the Western Front Way, by Anthony Seldon

Review by Gary Sheffield

Years ago, I read a collection of letters written by A.D. Gillespie, a young infantry officer killed in 1915. I've read many books of this sort, but what made this one stand out was Gillespie's suggestion that the belt of devastation along the Western Front should be turned into a path of peace. In 2021, Sir Anthony Seldon, inspired by this idea, walked along the length of the Western Front from the Swiss frontier to the Channel. This book is the story of this walk, and it is a joy to read. It is an intimate experience: the author is very candid about his health and state of mind. He was without a job and regarded his last one as a failure, he was mourning his wife, who had died of cancer, and was falling in love with someone else. In short, Seldon was going through a personal crisis.

The book is a combination of travelogue and history of the First World War, interspersed with Seldon's meditations. It is amusing – Seldon has a nicely self-deprecating tone, and frequently has mishaps – getting lost, locals not understanding his shaky French and even, rather alarmingly, being bitten by a fierce dog. It is also emotionally powerful. As Seldon readily admits, he has been profoundly affected by the Great War, and particularly by Douglas Gillespie's writings and vision. The humanity of both men shines through these pages.

Since we have been on a battlefield tour together, Anthony Seldon won't be surprised to find that I disagree with many of historical judgments. *Pace* Seldon, the evidence is clear that First World War generals did learn lessons from their mistakes and apply them to subsequent operations. Seldon's view that Haig should have ended the Passchendaele offensive in October 1917, was never realistic for excellent military and political reasons. Because Seldon walked the old front line, he did not visit the sites of the great Allied victories of 1918 such as Amiens, and the Hindenburg Line. Add these to the mix, and a rather different picture of the Western Front emerges.

'I struggle to see how the First World War served any useful purpose,' Seldon writes, 'certainly not commensurate' with the vast losses. The reality was that the 1914-18 War was one of aggression and conquest. At the end of the book, when he is in Belgium, Seldon glimpses this reality: he was, 'brought up on stories of the liberation of Western Europe from the Nazis... [but] the ending of the... [Great War] is new to me, and I marvel at the history as I walk through the scene of this earlier liberation'. Bad as the First World War was, it would have been even worse had Germany and its allies emerged victorious. The 1914-18 War was an appalling tragedy, but it wasn't futile. Putin's invasion of Ukraine is a reminder just how fragile 'peace' is, and that it requires security as well as the mere absence of war.

Anthony Seldon is a charming literary companion, and the ending of the book, with him newly married and back on track, is uplifting. *The Path of Peace* is hugely enjoyable. It is pleasing that all its profits will go the Western Front Way, set up to make Douglas Gillespie's vision of a Way of Peace come true. In these dark times, all signs of hope are very welcome.

Gary Sheffield is an acclaimed historian of World War One and author of *Forgotten Victory: The First World War Myths and Realities*.

The Mongol Storm: Making and Breaking Empires in the Medieval Near East

Review by Trevor James

In the West we tend to know that the Near East was over-run by Mongol forces towards the end of the period of the Crusades. The detail of what we know is generally very limited, whilst generally believing that Genghis Khan was at the heart of what took place.

What Nicholas Morton offers us is both a detailed narrative of how it happened and, very importantly, an analysis of the various elements involved in what became a serious challenge on the edges of Europe. In reading the book, wider parallels with our own times become apparent. He reveals that the various states and jurisdictions that comprise the Near East in its widest definition were more concerned with local rivalries and their own local security than they were with the impending threat that they were facing from the East.

Morton reveals a perspective on what happened by placing the Mongols at the centre of the story. We discover that the invaders were, in reality, the descendants of Genghis Khan, and we also discover, again in parallel with what has happened in our modern times when 'fake news' abounds, that some in the West mistakenly believed that the horse-riding invaders were somehow linked to the legendary figure of 'Prester John' and the notion that their arrival might represent a form of spiritual re-invigoration.

My instincts are always to seek to develop a framework to understand something as complex as the emergence of the Mongols as an historical phenomenon. Nicholas Morton closes by providing just that very necessary overarching framework, with a very clinical analysis of what happened, assisted by the observations of two contemporary commentators, Ibn Battuta and Ibn Khaldun. What he reveals is that, in essence, this was a clash between a pastoral culture which depended on endless movement and settled agricultural communities which depended on stability, the latter having created different forms of political leadership to support their way of life. This contrast was stark and the populations to the west did not understand the phenomenon that they were facing. Ironically, as time progressed, the Mongols began to adopt some of the political management techniques of the West and internal familial rivalries undermined the solidarity of their earlier emergence, both of which ultimately led to the decline of their power.

What the Mongols achieved, much as Alexander the Great had done more than a millennium previously, was to open up the Eurasian landmass and access in both directions became possible for traders and other travellers. This then itself created a transnational problem because it was this exposure, political as well as economic, that enabled the Black Death to spread so energetically and speedily from the east into western Europe in the late 1340s, with an international death toll of mind-blowing proportions. An extraordinary introduction to a highly transformative era in world history.

Trevor James is a historian and former Secretary of the Historical Association.

A Marriage of Fortune, by Anne O'Brien

Review by Ella Beales

Anne O'Brien is renowned for uncovering the voices of forgotten women in medieval history. *A Marriage of Fortune* is no exception, offering insight into female experiences of life in England during the War of the Roses and the early Tudor period.

This novel follows the Paston women: both those within the family, and those whose lives were irrevocably changed by their encounters with Paston men. Set between the 1460s and 1480s, this novel has been inspired by the 'Paston Letters' collection. O'Brien brings to life the Paston family with her captivating storytelling, using these letters as inspiration for the creation of a narrative in which medieval women are finally placed back at the centre of their own stories. She also brings awareness to the value of letters, Wills and other written documents, as enduring testaments of medieval women's lives.

A Marriage of Fortune predominantly follows Paston matriarch Margaret, her daughter Margery, and her son's love interest, Anne Haute. As Margaret navigates life as a widowed mother, she must battle against threats to her family's financial security. Refusing to allow her family's future to be determined by the policies and politics of men, Margaret feels her only way to protect the Paston legacy is to use her daughters to create advantageous marriage alliances. Her anger at her children jeopardising their property, prosperity and position in society with their choices, is tinged with her omnipresent fear that there will come a time when she will no longer be able to champion her children's future. Anne O'Brien masters this emotional balance beautifully.

Meanwhile, Margaret's eldest son, Sir John, needs only to legalise his marriage *per verba de presenti* to the Queen's cousin, Anne Haute, to change the fate of the Paston family. Yet, he seems unable to commit. Rather than focusing on Sir John's perspective, O'Brien offers a voice to another silenced woman in history: we witness the impact of Sir John's erratic behaviour on Anne's mental state, her perpetual uncertainty, her love and loathing for her betrothed, and her fear that history will forget her and her experiences if she isn't legally bound to Sir John.

Perhaps the most emotionally powerful narrative in *A Marriage of Fortune* is that of Margaret's daughter, Margery, who must choose whether to disregard her mother's ambitions for her and face being ostracised, when she falls in love with a man below her station. Following her decisions, her mother's tortured conscience, and the heartbreak and hope that ensues, this novel shows how a woman's status does not always have to be altered by the decisions of men: sometimes, a woman's reclaiming of her agency can change the lives of many.

Anne O'Brien is impressive in her intertwining of the Paston women's stories, showing the plethora of female experiences of marriage, love, desire, loss and motherhood during this period. Margaret Paston repeats the motto 'I am a woman of infinite resources' when faced with seemingly impossible odds. Her resilience, and that of her fellow female protagonists, is the enduring legacy of this novel.

Ella Beales is a Historical Researcher, Archivist and Public Historian.

Speed, Aggression, Surprise: The Untold Secret Origins of the SAS, by Tom Petch

Review by Gavin Mortimer

Dudley Clarke has had a rough time of it in recent years. He made the headlines in 2010 when photos were published of him in the national press wearing women's clothes, pictures that were taken by Spanish police in 1941 when he was arrested in Madrid.

Three years later this incident was back in the news when the National Archives declassified a selection of its files: 'Dudley Clarke: The cross-dressing spy who was arrested on a secret mission,' was the headline in the Independent.

More recently, Clarke made a few fleeting appearances in the BBC wartime drama, *SAS Rogue Heroes*, loosely based on the formation of the Special Air Service in 1941. Dominic West clearly had fun bringing out Clarke's eccentricity, as well as his stockings and mascara.

Fortunately, Tom Petch has written a book that for serious students of the Second World War reveals that while Clarke had his foibles, he was an audacious and unorthodox thinker at a time when the British army was, in the words of David Stirling, full of 'fossilised shits'.

Stirling, who founded the SAS in the summer of 1941, features prominently in *Speed, Aggression, Surprise: The Untold Secret Origins of the SAS*. Petch, a former troop commander of 22SAS, explains how Clarke's subliminal methods were put into practice by the SAS. To do that, Petch selected an unsung member of the original SAS, Lt Bill Fraser, and follows him throughout the war, as he fights his way from North Africa through Europe into Germany. 'They were opposite ends of a spectrum,' writes Petch. 'Clarke, the master of the subliminal methods, and Fraser, the very sharp end of those methods.'

Though they never met Clarke and Fraser had much in common; they were lonely men, outsiders by nature. For both, the war was a Godsend, an opportunity for adventure and an escape from a world of conventions in which neither felt comfortable.

As Petch skilfully recounts, Clarke, a film-buff, harnessed his imagination early on in his military career to great effect, pioneering his 'subliminal methods' to deceive the enemy into believing something was going to happen when it was not. The key to Clarke's success was his realisation that 'military operations and theatrical productions are closely related'. He first combined the two in 1935 when he spooked an audience in Aden who were watching a mock battle as part of King George V's Silver Jubilee celebrations. So realistic had the battle been that the audience thought they were being attacked by Italians. 'Placing fear in the minds of this audience was a successful demonstration of his subliminal methods,' writes Petch.

Five years later Clarke was sent by the War Office to Norway to deploy his subliminal methods against Germany. It was the start of a remarkable career that included a hand in Operation Mincemeat and Operation Copperhead, the latter involving despatching a Bernard Montgomery lookalike to Algiers shortly before D-Day in the hope of confusing the Germans.

The book's title is misleading. It is more about Clarke than the SAS, and so it should be. Their story has been told so many times that there is little left to say. Not so Clarke's, and Petch's book is a fascinating study of a complex and innovative man who deserves to be remembered as far more than a cross-dresser.

Gavin Mortimer is a historian of the British Special Forces, and author of the acclaimed *David Stirling, The Phoney Major: The Life, Times and Truth about the Founder of the SAS.*

Bellatrix, by S.J.A.Turney

Review by Peter Tonkin

Bellatrix is the second of Simon Turney's brilliant new *Legion XXII* historical adventure novels.

It follows on directly from the first, *The Capsarius* (which incidentally has one of the most gripping openings I have read recently). Equally enthralling, this follows legionary capsarius or doctor Titus Cervianus, with his tent-mates, his cohort and his legion, the Twenty Second Deiotariana, on their dramatic journey south out of Aegyptus and into the hinterland of Kush, modern Sudan. Facing the legion is the Bellatrix of the title, Amanirenus, the Kandake or Warrior Queen, with her vast armies, willing to go to any length to rid their land of the Roman invaders. A desire soon intensified beyond measure by the Romans' casual slaughter of local villagers as well as of their priests; followed by desecration and outright destruction of their holiest temples. Acts which horrify Cervianus, the conscience of the cohort, and which he is swift to try and repair. Also working very effectively as an ally is the terrain in which Cervianus and his companions find themselves. But the more the Romans endure and achieve, the greater the odds against them become.

There are several elements which raise this book and its predecessor so high. There is Titus Cervianus himself. He is brilliantly engaging. He is a doctor, and a good one. His mind-set (at first at least) is that of a rational observer. As he himself announces, 'I've always been a man of reason.' And so he is to begin with. But the fact that he makes that observation during a conversation he is holding with a statue of Sobel the Crocodile God, illustrates that the experiences he endures are changing him. He is vividly aware of his own short-comings and is all the more likeable for that. His tent mates look after him (obviously they rely on him if hurt or wounded) and put up with the fact he is not a very good soldier: at one point he actually, unwisely, throws his sword at an enemy. His unsoldierly actions and often naive observations add to his appeal and leaven the occasionally gruesome narrative with humour.

The desert inland of the Nile is fearsomely well presented with its burning days and freezing nights, its unseen dangers - snakes and scorpions - and larger hazards like sandstorms and black-robed headhunters all of which grip the reader further while decimating the characters.

Many of the soldiers who set out alongside their capsarius do not make it into the ever-deepening danger at his side. And this is even before the Warrior Queen sends her army to destroy them all. This is historical storytelling at its best, brilliantly researched, full of convincing and engaging characters and gripping action. The settings are also terrifically well done. The geographical setting as mentioned above; but also the historical setting, as one would expect from the author of the *Marius Mules* series, to which *The Capsarius* and *Bellatrix* make a fantastic addition.

Peter Tonkin is a novelist and the author of the *Caesar's Spies* series.

The Jaggard Case, by J.C.Briggs

Review by Allan Martin

JC Briggs brings the reader into the world of mid-nineteenth-century London very effectively indeed. *The Jaggard Case* is the tenth in Briggs' series of crime novels featuring the writer as detective, which began with *The Murder of Patience Brooke* in 2014. The mystery begins with a disappearance: Dickens' friend, and co-investigator, Superintendent Sam Jones of Scotland Yard, has taken on, on Dickens's recommendation, an orphan girl, Posy, as a housemaid. One weekend Posy goes with a maid from a nearby household, Phoebe, to visit the latter's family, who live in a cottage on the edge of the city. On Monday the two girls do not reappear. Superintendent Jones, and Dickens, fear the worst, that the girls have been abducted to be forced into sex slavery in a brothel, and set out to find them. Their investigations lead them to suspect a link with forger, suspected murderer and master-criminal Martin Jaggard. However, every time they think they are close to him another body or two turns up, and Jaggard moves on. Eventually however, there must come a confrontation…

I've not read any of the other books in the series, so I came to this one with an open mind, apart from a raised eyebrow over Charles Dickens as a detective. But I soon got used to him. It's clear from the book, as well as what I found on the author's website, that Ms Briggs has done a great deal of research, not only on Dickens himself, but on the world he inhabited, both the circles in which he moved, and the less salubrious aspects of the metropolis, in which he was deeply interested. The transitions between these worlds work because the author is able to conjure up powerful images of the reality of life in the decaying slums, and characters that work in those settings. That includes Dickens too, who functions more as a co-ordinator and team leader than as the eccentric genius detective the author could have been tempted to portray; and this makes him believable. He doesn't seek to hog the limelight or constantly tell people about himself or his latest book, and thus doesn't become a distraction from the onward progress of the plot.

Would it have been as good without Charles Dickens as a central character, with some other detective conjured up by the writer? I have to say that the restrained use which Jean Briggs makes of him enables him, for me at least, to function, not as a gimmick, but as an enhancement to the book.

The Jaggard Case is a good read, with a well-thought-out plot, strong characters, and settings that lean out of the text to enfold you. And J. C. Briggs can write, too; her use of language enables the book to flow so well that you can't help just starting to read the next chapter.

Allan Martin is the author of *Blood Winter*.

The Fortune Keeper, by Deborah Swift

Review by Amie Bawa

The novel centres on the curious Mia Caiozzi who has a passion for astrology. Mia's thirst for knowledge springs the novel into adventure – she is desperate to seek answers amongst the planets and stars; answers that may guide her during the course of her life or lend themselves to the past.

At a time when Italy was entering its scientific awakening, such abstract ideas and theories were in conflict with the beliefs of the Catholic Church. The prosecution of Galileo Galilei, for his 'absurd' astrological teachings, is an echo in the back of Mia's mind. Due to this danger, and the threat of the Inquisition, Mia must study in secret.

Mia resides in the Jewish ghetto of Venice with her step-parents, Giulia and Fabio. Giulia and Fabio are both determined to keep a low-profile and live a quiet life in order to escape the repercussions of Giuila's notorious past.

Mia soon comes to the realisation that she knows very little about her step-parents pasts and their reasons for moving to Venice. Feeling like an outsider in her family, Mia longs to be a part of high and noble society and to become a successful astrologer. While the reader may root for Mia's bid for independence, it also gives rise to a rebellious nature, resulting in selfish and impulsive decisions. All too soon, Mia and Giuila's webs of secrets collide, raising the question – does history repeat itself?

Despite the allure of the shimmering canals of Venice, Mia is quickly caught in the city's dark and unforgiving shadows as Giulia's past creeps back to haunt her family. Brother Mario returns with a vengeance and is determined to get his hands on the elusive Giuila, who murdered his brother using her deadly poison Aqua Tofana.

In seeking justice for his brother, the enigmatic Imbroglio is employed to carry out the dirty work. Well-versed in the art of assassination, Imbroglio is masked by his alter-ego, Signor Moretti – a wealthy and intelligent nobleman. It is this persona that Mia quickly becomes enraptured by, after bumping into Moretti at a lecture. Through Mia and Moretti's encounters, Swift successfully builds tension and maintains a gripping, fast-paced storyline.

Swift's ability to create a vivid and immersive setting of Renaissance Italy, through detailed grandeur of architecture, flowing canals, and the bustling city, is also what makes this a captivating tale. The array of elements; tension, excitement, grief, and political intrigue, make *The Fortune Keeper* a must read for both existing fans of the series, and all historical fiction readers.

Amie Bawa was formerly an Editorial Assistant at Aspects of History

The Dark History of Gin, by Mike Rendell

Review by Chantelle Lee

Gin may be at the heart of Mike Rendell's new book, but this is in fact a wide-reaching history that intersects with a broad range of social, political and cultural topics. Each chapter takes us through the development and evolution of gin throughout the centuries, beginning with the medicinal uses of juniper berries in Ancient Greece and Rome, and ending with a discussion of gin in twentieth and twenty-first century cinema and in our cultural psyche. Along the way, Rendell covers the links with alchemy, how gin has been variously encouraged and discouraged by law, its association with social unrest, and the birth of the cocktail. Although he largely focuses on English and British history, Rendell does touch upon gin in international context, from the United States to the Philippines. An array of well-known historical figures, from Catherine de Medici to Al Capone, are also interwoven into the narrative. All of this comes together to support Rendell's argument that gin has a fascinating history and has been centre stage in many key historical events.

In many ways, this is indeed a 'dark' history. Rendell sensitively explores the drink's more sinister side, spending several chapters discussing gin's associations with Georgian drunkenness and the effect of alcoholism on the urban poor. There are some truly tragic stories involving alcohol-induced child neglect and criminality. Likewise, there are some interesting reflections on gender, with gin being linked to prostitution and women more generally being seen as the most susceptible to the 'evils of drink'. Gin frequently played a role in some of the violent expressions of unrest, such as in the 1780 Gordon Riots, which saw a Catholic distillery attacked. Rendell follows these chapters with discussions on the growth of temperance movements in the lead up to Prohibition, examining Victorian morality and efforts to curtail excessive drinking.

However, this is also a wittily-written volume and there are plenty of interesting and often humorous anecdotes to complement the more serious sections. These are often in the form of the many attempts to circumvent gin and alcohol-related laws, demonstrating century-spanning determination to enjoy a drink. Some of the most fascinating examples include 'Puss and Mew shops' in the mid-eighteenth century: to bypass laws restricting the sale of gin, sellers would distribute the gin to patrons from behind the sign of a cat. Equally interesting is the discussion of Prohibition speakeasies; in New York alone, there were double the amount of speakeasies than there had been saloons before the Eighteenth Amendment. The book also ends with an impressively long list of synonyms and slang for gin, along with a collection of early gin cocktail recipes for those who have been inspired.

Rendell does a superb job of weaving an impressive amount of detail into this relatively short book, without it ever feeling over-saturated. His book is an excellent example of a highly effective micro history and is a must-read, not only for those interested in the history of gin, but in social and cultural history more broadly.

Chantelle Lee is an Editorial Assistant at Aspects of History

Agent in the Shadows, by Alex Gerlis

Review by David Boyle

Well, I don't know about you, but I thought Jack Miller and Sophia von Naundorf had made it through to peacetime at the end of *Agent in Peril.*

Not a bit of it – they still have their most exciting and dangerous mission before them, and what could be their most effective operation.

But, thinking about it you couldn't really end a successful franchise like 'Wolf Pack Spies' after just two books. So you will be glad to hear that Jack and Sophia are back – though I have to say that I had become so fond of them in the previous two books, that I was a little scared for them both as I opened the latest Gerlis.

This time, much of the action takes place in Berne in Switzerland – where the agents and their British handlers are based – and in Lyons, where Klaus Barbie, the so-called 'Butcher' of that city has taken up residence.

The opportunity emerges for Sophia to impersonate a senior Gestapo representative on Barbie's staff, so she really has to take it. Only this time, while she is searching the archives for clues about who betrayed Jean Moulin – de Gaulle's representative, trying to unite a disparate resistance movement - in June 1943, they also find that their arrangements and cover-stories are less well-organised than before, because there is also a mole in among the British handlers in Berne.

This leads to the unexpected death of one of the best-loved British spy masters. I won't give it away or be a spoiler by saying who it is.

There is something about the way that Alex Gerlis writes that makes these books so compelling. His prose is sparse – there are few, if any, judgements about the terrifying world he is describing – but you learn to like many of the characters.

And especially Jack – an American sports writer – and Sophia, the widow of a senior SS officer, who had both become British spies.

And the British are portrayed as you might expect – terribly, terribly public school and only completely at ease with each other when they went to the same schools, or their fathers knew each other. Yet you somehow love them for it anyway.

There are only a handful of historically real characters in the book, and only Barbie is actually at the heart of the action. He is much younger than anyone expects, as befits a man who lived to be convicted of crimes against humanity in Lyons, as late as 1987.

Yet the events that are described as the background to the book, and the techniques which were used by spies – and the dreadful decisions they had to take in order to survive in wartime – are all highly accurate and authentic.

Gerlis has done his research. Though he says at the end of the book that, even in fictional form, the issue of who is Source Armand, the identity of whoever betrayed Jean Moulin, is still so fraught in France that he was twice warned off writing about it.

For that fact alone, this book is worth adding to your collection.

David Boyle is a novelist and the author of *Xanthe Schneider Enigma Files*.

Jamie MacGillivray: A Renegade's Journey, by John Sayles

Review by Oliver Webb-Carter

The Seven Years War should be fertile ground for novelists, with so many belligerents involved, fighting on multiple continents and in landscapes that invoke drama and possibility it should be like the Napoleonic era. Churchill called it the 'first world war' so it's strange therefore, that there are probably only two well-known novels, *The Last of the Mohicans* by James Fenimore Cooper, and *The Luck of Barry Lyndon* by William Makepeace Thackeray. The former is set among the mighty forests of upstate New York, and of course features Native American tribes who are allied with the British and French forces in the colonies of North America. John Sayles' latest novel opens at the scene of a great defeat by another native race, the Highlanders at the Battle of Culloden in 1746. The result of Culloden was the destruction of much of Highland culture, and Jamie MacGillivray, a minor aristocrat from the clan MacGillivray, as a result of the catastrophic defeat, is shipped to America, having cheated death twice, to work as a slave in the colony of Maryland.

This being an epic novel, we follow MacGillivray from the '45 all the way through to the conclusion of the French & Indian War nearly 13 years later as Jamie mixes with African slaves, European immigrants and particularly Native American tribes that are constantly being buffeted by the insatiable hunger for land from the French and British prior to the outbreak of war in 1756 – the cause of which was a blundering George Washington, who makes an ambitious appearance. Sayles has captured the environment beautifully in those early years as America is formed, but also conveys the almost anarchic nature of the frontier.

MacGillivray is not the only character we follow, as Jenny Ferguson is also caught up in the post-Culloden Highland-phobic fever which saw Highland dress and Erse proscribed. After surviving a brutal assault, she fares slightly better than her countryman and is befriended by a kindly French officer, who is born in Martinique and reminded of the fact by brother officers.

Meanwhile MacGillivray has been taken in by the Lenape, whose chief, Shingas, causes mayhem to colonial and British interests in the lead up to, and during the French-Indian War. He allies with the French against Britain, which pleases MacGillivray no end. His gift of languages makes him invaluable as we follow the various diplomatic wrangles between personalities: Shingas (the Terrible) of course, but so too the 'Half-King' Tanacharison, the aforementioned Washington, James Braddock and finally the brilliant James Wolfe. As one reads of tribes such as the Lenape, Ottowa, Mohawk, Shawnee and Odawa one is aware of what happens more than 100 years later, and the experience, much like those Highland clans, is one that stays with the reader throughout. There are 18th century characters throughout that makes this novel such a joy to read, including William Hogarth, James Wolfe, the Marquis de Montcalm and wonderful turn from Lord Lovat, the 'Auld Fox'.

In *Jamie MacGillivray* John Sayles has written a masterpiece that holds the reader in a vice-like grip and refuses to release until the final page.

Oliver Webb-Carter is the Editor of Aspects of History.

Next Issue

Martyn Rady on Middle Kingdoms of Europe

Tessa Dunlop on Elizabeth II and the new Carolingian Age

Peter Taylor on the Troubles

Alice Loxton on Gillray and Cartoonists of the 19th century

Printed in Great Britain
by Amazon

23913284R00044